Table of Contents

FOREWORD

This book is the story of the greater part of my life.

I was extremely lucky to stumble, back in 1965, into the infancy of plastics on automobiles, and to be part of the following 50 years that were the most productive in the development and advancement of plastic materials on cars and trucks.

It would be impossible to meet today's stringent fuel standards without the weight advantage that plastic parts and products provide on our automobiles!

I believe the story of how plastics conquered Detroit's – and later the world's – automotive industry needs to be told.

In telling the story, I avoided most surnames of my automotive contacts to, as they say, protect the innocent (and, as my attorney advised, to protect me from being sued).

I intend no harm, but there were a lot of characters in and around the industry, and they all contributed in one way or another to this revolution.

All events and dates are as accurate as my memory, aided by my trusted Day Timers of over 30 years, allowed me to put to paper.

I cannot thank my wife Ursula enough for her help in writing this book, and for the patience she had with me in preserving my Day Timers against her ardent desire to get rid of them. Without them, this story could never have been written.

Peter Herrmann, July 2017

CHAPTER 1: Birthing An Industry

I woke up with someone banging inside my head, wanting to get out. The sun from the window was burning a trail across my forehead as I tried to get up. What time is it? What happened?

The room, I recognized, was my living room. I looked around in my haze and saw on the floor two Molson Export beer cases and an empty bottle of a single-malt Irish whiskey. Then I noticed a guy passed out in the small corner between the kitchen and the laundry room.

It was Frank, an immigrant who had been recently hired at North American Plastic, where I work. Frank liked alcohol like a fish likes water; and, as we later found out, he was not a person to be trusted.

After a little while my head stopped hurting and I started to remember what happened. The two of us had celebrated the birth of my daughter Karin, born the previous day at Sydenham Hospital in Wallaceburg, Ontario, Canada.

Karin is the second child born to Ursula and me. Andrew, our first child, had been born two years earlier in Sarnia, a town about 30 miles to the north, where Lake Huron empties into the Saint Clair River and flows toward Detroit, Michigan and Windsor, Ontario, and then on to Lake Erie.

This area of Canada is magnificent and I am glad we settled here after coming from Germany nine years earlier.

The day is May 19, 1966. I had managed to get a job as decorating foreman a year ago at North American Plastic (NAP).

NAP is a privately owned American company, making plastic parts for the "Big Three" auto companies – (Ford, Chrysler, and General Motors). The company's facility had been built between 1964 and 1966. The early NAFTA agreement (North American Free Trade Agreement) was starting to work out well between the U.S. and Canada and, as we now know, many years later with Mexico.

Mike Ladney, then the owner of Detroit Plastic Molding (DPM), an established automotive plastic parts supplier, had built the NAP plant in Wallaceburg to take advantage of the new NAFTA legislation allowing automotive parts to be transferred tax-free between the U.S. and Canada.

This is about an hour's drive across the border (and the Saint Clair River) from the Detroit plant on 10 Mile Road, just east of Gratiot Avenue.

Though both companies made the same parts, on some jobs the lower labor and fixed costs at NAP gave DPM a significant cost-advantage over its competitors.

I had been hired on the 15th of January 1965, and I will thank the good Lord for this to my dying day.

The previous year, I had invested all that I had into a small machinery repair shop in Wallaceburg. I had called the shop Five Star, for reasons I no longer remember.

Five Star's equipment consisted of two lathes, one shaper, a mill, some benders, ark and acetylene welding equipment, and lots of square and round metal rods. The main revenue-generating business was repairing farm equipment.

This business seemed like a good idea at the time. There were many farms in the area and plenty of work, as farm equipment gets damaged in the fields during the year. Lots of axles, shafts, bearings, rims, pulleys, and God knows how many other parts are damaged in the normal course of using them and need to be repaired or replaced.

However, there was one problem that I had been too naïve to discern ahead of time. Farmers get paid after they have sold their harvest in the fall of the year. And only after they get paid do they have money to pay the people they owe.

I had bought the shop late in 1963 with every penny that I could scrape together, and by the time our son Andrew was born the following May, Ursula and I were in a financial mess. As I stated before, there was plenty of work; I could have worked 20 hours a day if I wanted to. But there was never a regular income. Money was just not coming in on a timely basis.

"I promise I will pay you next month or later in the fall, when I get paid and have money," was what I heard most of the time from the farmers. "You know I am good for it," was the other line I heard a lot of times! But later in the fall a lot of these farmers moved to their winter quarters in Florida, and sometimes they forgot they owed money to people who had served them during the previous year.

It became obvious to Ursula that we could not survive on those promises and under their delayed payment plan system.

So, when North American Plastic advertised for management positions in the local newspaper, Ursula found a way to get me an interview with Bob Grimm, a German engineer who had been hired as their new plant manager and was in charge of hiring core employees.

Construction of the factory had begun and the plant was scheduled to be fully operational in the spring of 1966.

Mike Ladney's management people were hiring six people to be trained at their 10 Mile Road plant and, after a four-month training period, to start the manufacturing phase in Wallaceburg around the middle of 1966.

The positions they were looking to fill were three molding room supervisors, two decorating foremen, and one engineer.

The original hires were Emil Jacab, Henry Blondia, and Tom Kirby for the molding room; George McFadden as maintenance engineer; and Steve Lemak and me as decorating foremen.

CHAPTER 2: Falling in Love (With Plastics) - 20-25 lbs.

Right from the start I liked working with plastic and — as crazy as it sounds — I liked the smell.

The four other men being trained to run the Canadian side of the business were the aforementioned Henry Blondia and Emil Jacab, as well as two guys named Tom and Steve. Along with Bob Grimm, the plant manager, we all drove to Detroit Plastic Molding (DPM) every day for four months. We drove up to Sombra, took the ferry to Marine City, and then drove the Marine City Highway to I-94, then west to the 10 Mile Road exit and on to the plant.

There we learned injection molding and decorating plastic parts from the best and most knowledgeable people in the business at the time.

I remember the plastic smell when I arrived at the 10 Mile Road plant for the first time, and the sight of the enormous molding machines.

There were 23 of them in the molding room, ranging from 450 to 1200 tons; as well as some small arbor presses.

The decorating room with the 2 flow coaters, 6 metalizing chambers, and 12 Decca paint booths overwhelmed me because everything appeared so technical.

Everywhere I looked there were plastic parts being conveyed through the plant at ceiling level on conveyor chains, from the molding machines to the flow coater, to the metallizing chambers; then on to a number of different paint booths, depending on the painting needs of the part.

The finished "metalized" parts came out shiny, as if they were chrome-plated. The parts were then painted, assembled, and packed for shipping to car assembly plants.

At that time, in 1966, automotive plastic parts were limited to small instrument clusters or dials, armrests, heater ducts, and outlets for the interior of the car. I estimate that there were between 20 to 25 pounds of plastic used on the average American-made car.

DPM at this time made and delivered plastic parts to Ford Motor for the Comet, Falcon, and Mustang models; General Motors for their Pontiac, Oldsmobile, and Buick models; and Chrysler for their sedan and Barracuda models.

For me it was wonderful seeing all these shiny and colorful plastic auto parts being made. I felt immediately that I had found the work of my life. From that very first day, I was hooked.

Mike Ladney, the owner, had an uncanny ability to find and motivate talented people to help him run and, more important to him, grow his company.

A few of the people I met when I began my training on January 15, 1966, were named Rudy, Bill, and Hugh. Rudy, a big guy over 6-feet tall, was one of the best injection-molding experts in the Detroit area.

Bill was a top-notch chemical engineer and the ultimate talent in decorating on plastic, from interior decorating, painting, and hot stamping to later becoming a pioneer and an ace in chrome plating on plastic. He was also the one that took me under his wing, and he helped me tremendously throughout my time at DPM.

Hugh was also a German transplant, and he was a wizard in mold making and design. He ran our mold-making plant, Paragon Tools, in Windsor, Canada.

The team of Dick, Lynn, Will, Gene and Bill Mc. could design and engineer complicated, never-before-done processes to make a product more cost-effective, which kept DPM way ahead of our competition.

Vic was my training supervisor in the decorating department. From him I learned the fine art of making plastic look pretty and, just as importantly, how to get the most out of workers. (I quickly learned that was not achieved by being mean or overly aggressive!)

Pete and Bill were DPM's chief operating and chief financial officers. Pete ran the "day to day" operations with Mike's help.

Mike was starting to be busy traveling to Europe and Asia, trying to hook us up with other companies and/or to sell them our know-how. But that did not keep him from staying in touch on a daily basis by phone, or through our newly purchased fax machine.

In 1966, DPM's annual sales to the Big Three auto companies were close to $30 million, and they employed about 500 people, mostly women, in a well-run, 24-hour, three-shift operation.

It is interesting to note that at that time there were more than 30 plastic injection-molding companies located in the Detroit area alone — and all were fighting for the same plastics business from the Big Three.

There was Jim Robbins, Mercury, May, O'Sullivan, Regal, United, Prince, Continental, ABC Plastic, Delta, Royal, and Key Plastic, to name just a few of them.

Detroit was the place to be if you wanted to be in this business. All factions of the car companies were right there: purchasing, engineering, and styling; and you had to be at their doorstep every single day fighting for new business and defending the business you had!

As I quickly learned, DPM was already highly regarded by the purchasing and engineering departments of all the big auto companies. Mike Ladney's DPM was known as the "We can do it" company.

If another company got into trouble, and that happened more often than I thought possible, DPM received a call from one of the purchasing departments for help.

An explanation here: When a part is placed to bid, potential suppliers quote on a piece price for the part and also on the tooling costs needed to make the part. The successful bidder is responsible for procuring the tools at his own expense. He is paid for the tools when the part is approved for production.

After that, the tools are the property of the car company, and they can move them anywhere they need to in case that company has problems delivering parts.

DPM's people would go into the plant that had the problem, no matter what time of day or night. We used our own DPM trucks to pick up all the tools and bring them to the 10 Mile Road plant.

Rudy, with his crew and his engineers, managed every time to have that new job running the very next day and we would then be the ones shipping parts to the auto company's assembly plant (including weekends or holidays) from our 10 Mile plant!

That earned DPM the respect of all the car companies, and we made friends at the various purchasing and engineering departments. This willingness to go the extra mile helped us survive during these turbulent times and DPM grew very fast from then on.

It was smart of Mike to build the 10 Mile Road plant on a 20 plus-acre site between Gratiot and Kelly, with ample space for expansion towards the 11 Mile Road.

CHAPTER 3: Getting to America - My Story

Now, I think that I need to get to some details of my background.

I was born on September 20, 1936, in Wuppertal, Germany.

By 1943, World War II had started to affect us. Wuppertal, an industrial town and the founding home of the Bayer Factories, had become a bombing target. My family – my mother, Hertha, my one-year old sister Brigitte, and myself – became homeless after our house was hit and destroyed by a bomb. My father, who was driving ammunition to the German soldiers at Stalingrad at that time, was allowed to come home to help us relocate to a safer area – Lauscha, a small town in the hills of Thuringia.

I don't remember much of the trip; I was only six years old. But I know we stopped in Sonneberg to change trains to get us into the mountains and later that evening we arrived at the Hotel Fridolin in Lauscha.

We were about 50 displaced people, and we were auctioned off – I can't think of another word – to a public that did not want us.

But because of the decree by the German Reich, the people of Lauscha had to take us in.

We were dead tired after a daylong train ride with an uncertain future, and hungry and thirsty to boot. Some official read off names to the local people in the room and, family-by-family, we left with our new hosts. My mother, Brigitte, and I were the last ones whose names were read.

Nathan Greiner Nandele, who was a teacher at the public school in Lauscha, said that he would take the mother and the little girl but that he did not have room for a boy. Finally, a woman whose name I have since forgotten took me until other arrangements could be made.

I was tired, still hungry, and for the first time alone; and I was in a strange bed in very strange surroundings. It was incredibly dark that night. I had always been in a big city where some lights are always on. But Lauscha was in a valley in the middle of the mountains, with only millions of pine and spruce trees of Thuringia all around me.

In the town of fewer than 8,000 people, it somehow took over a week to reunite me with my mother and Brigitte. But we were eventually assigned a one-bedroom apartment with a living room and kitchen on "Alter Weg" 19.

The living room had a three-tier high tiled masonry oven to heat the place, right out of a picture book, almost like in Hansel and Gretel's "Hexenhaus." My sister Brigitte and I sat in our pajamas on one of the ledges of the oven in the wintertime, staying cozy and warm up there.

The downside of this place in our eyes was that it had no water-powered toilet. What we did have was an old fashioned outhouse down the hall, leading into the back of the house where the pit was.

This became tolerable in the summer, fall, and winter. But in the spring, when this thing needed to be emptied and the contents distributed onto the surrounding fields, the pit got to be awfully full, and there were a lot of things moving in there.

When it almost reached the top, it became an easy decision for me to change my location to go to the "bathroom" and do my business in the nearby, nicely overgrown, school gardens. And I don't think anybody ever was the wiser.

The really good news was that we never saw any more war action.

No more air raid alarms in the middle of the night, or burning houses to see or smell after the all clear was sounded and we came out of the shelters. But most important, there were no more crying women and children after we moved to Lauscha.

The following years there were spent making new friends and we felt good and safe in our home in Thuringia.

Lauscha was a glass blower's town. An independent artist lived and worked in every house or flat, blowing glass figurines or animal figures or Christmas ornaments of every kind, which they sold throughout the world.

I watched in awe for hours as figurines were blown and formed by the hundreds, to be put in white cardboard boxes to be shipped.

But Christmas ornaments were their specialty. I remember fanciful, all silvery, decorated Christmas trees in every household in Lauscha. (It was their tradition, at the stroke of midnight on New Years Eve, to toss these beautifully decorated spruce trees with all this ornamental glass out the windows onto the snow!)

Glass eyes were another specialty of some talented townspeople. During the war years, I saw many one-eyed soldiers come into town by train, and leave a few days later with two eyes, looking as if nothing bad had ever happened to them.

I still have a few examples of Lauscha craftsmanship in a drawer at my house.

My mother made friends easily. She was helpful and became sought after for advice because she came from a big city and spoke the High German language so well!

Most people in Lauscha spoke with a dialect that only they could understand. And theirs was different from the dialect in Ernsthal, only about 6 miles away; and again different from the people's dialect in Hasenthal, in another valley about 10 miles away.

After the war ended in 1945, the Russians arrived and occupied that area of Thuringia, remaining there until the Berlin Wall came down in 1989.

❆❆❆

My father made it through the War without being wounded and was captured by British soldiers in Holland. He was imprisoned for a short time there and only came to us in Lauscha early in 1946.

He never got close to the people of Lauscha or the friends my mother had made. They considered him a dandy because, no matter the weather, he always wore a suit and tie, and highly polished shoes. He did not fit into the simple mountain life of Thuringia.

But mother and father got along well and on the second of November 1949 my sister Barbara was born at the hospital in Sonneberg.

Early in 1950, my father could stand it no longer; he'd had enough of the small town life in the new "German Democratic Republic." He said goodbye to us and secretly crossed the border between Sonneberg and Coburg to go back to West Germany.

His goal was to reestablish his business as an independent textile salesman.

That left my mother, Brigitte, baby Barbara, and me in the hands of the German Communists.

I would like to say here that later in life I always regretted not having known my father better. But under the circumstances – I had been three years old when he was drafted and ten years old when he returned; and then he left us again when I was thirteen – there was little time for bonding between the two of us!

⌘⌘⌘

In May of 1950 my basic schooling came to its natural end in Lauscha. I finished the 8th grade, all the schooling required at that time in Germany. I had always been a pretty good student and hoped to continue with high school, then go on to a university for further study.

Unfortunately, I got caught up in the politics of the time.

My mother was warned that I could only enter the higher education program if she was willing to divorce my father.

(Anyone leaving the German Democratic Republic illegally was a deserter and considered an enemy of the state.)

At a meeting, which I was required to attend, the divorce papers had already been prepared and were on the table ready for my mother's signature. She could not bring herself to sign, and so I was denied a university education.

I was instead entered into a three-year apprenticeship program as a machine fitter at a former Siemens plant in Sonneberg, a town located about 25 miles to the south of Lauscha.

That was the punishment!

My apprenticeship program started at the end of summer in 1950. I was not yet fourteen years old, and I was relatively small for my age at barely five foot two inches tall.

"I am not ready," I told everyone. But nobody cared; I had to learn how to become a machine fitter.

I think that in today's "politically correct" climate this would be considered child labor and the Human Rights Commission would probably have a field day. But in 1950, in East Germany, that was the way things were done.

I did not want to be a machine fitter and hated every day of the three-year apprenticeship. I hated my dirty hands and fingernails and the oil-soaked and smelly clothes associated with the job. I hated the fact that as an apprentice or "stift" in German you had to do all the demeaning jobs the supervisors heaped on you.

To make matters worse, I had to get on the train in Lauscha around six o'clock in the morning and did not return until seven in the evening, six days a week.

And I never embraced the idea of fixing machines as a career. I felt I could do something more useful with my life. But under the Communist system, I had no choice but to obey; so I worked diligently at it, knowing in my heart that I would leave as soon as I was able to. I finished my apprenticeship in March of 1953 with excellent marks.

The upside was the theoretical education that I got from the apprenticeship program. I received good basic engineering lectures and these helped me greatly in my classes at the Maschinenbau Hoch Schule (Machine Builders University) when we returned to Wuppertal.

When the apprenticeship ended I was sixteen years old and I wanted to leave East Germany in the worst way possible.

By the middle of April, I managed to convince my mother to sell all our belongings and leave Lauscha for good.

⌘⌘⌘

In the early morning of April 14ᵗʰ, my mother, my two sisters, and I left Lauscha on a train heading for East Berlin. We had to change trains in Saalfeld, and there two nuns joined us and shared our train compartment. They took us under their wings (no pun intended) and vouched for us with the East German Police Patrol.

I remember the bombed-out buildings and the ruins of East Berlin as we stared out from the train. I thought at the time that it was a shame it still looked that bad eight years after the War had ended!

At the East German main station we switched to a subway train – at that time still running – on an adjacent track. On that subway we crossed the border into West Berlin.

We were free again!

A little explanation here: after the War ended in 1945, Berlin was divided into four sectors (one for each of the victors). The subway system served all citizens of Berlin and they could use the subway to visit relatives or go about their business. This arrangement ended in 1961 when the East Germans built the Wall.

In 1953 when we left it was still relatively easy to use the subway to cross into a Western section. However, after 1954 the East German State added more police patrols at the railway stations and on the trains to spot and catch potential deserters.

We stayed for approximately four weeks at a refugee camp near the Tempelhof Airport where I was once again separated from my mother and sister, and moved to a building that was occupied by men only.

We were finally declared "'Fluechtlinge' (refugees) returning home" and were flown by the Allied "Rosinen (Raisin) Bomber Bridge," to Hanover, West Germany.

We reunited with my father in Wuppertal a few weeks later. He had by then reestablished himself. And so, we were back in Wuppertal after an absence of 10 years.

Back in Wuppertal I found work right away at Bemberg, a nylon and perlon yarn producer (my very first venture into plastics), repairing machines and equipment onsite.

I was the youngest fully-qualified machine fitter in West Germany at the time and was paid well. I saved all the money I earned and in the fall started to attend evening classes at the Machine Builders University (Maschinenbau Hochschule) in Wuppertal five nights a week while working during the day at my job. Four years later, in the summer of 1957, I finished school with an engineering degree.

During the summer of 1955 I met Ursula Koetting, who was working as an apprentice in the office of my supervisor at Bemberg. Bemberg had a very good and well supervised youth group program, with weekly dances, table tennis and chess groups; and I joined them as often as my busy work/school schedule allowed it.

Ursula and I began to enjoy each other's company, and we participated in two, two-week long vacation trips organized by the Bemberg Youth Group, the first one in 1955 and the other in 1956.

The first trip took us to the Island of Sylt in the North Sea, and the following year we traveled to the Schlei, a contributing river to the Baltic Sea.

Sometime during that period Ursula and I fell in love, got secretly engaged, and decided to marry. We married (against the wishes of our parents) on September 20, 1957, my 21st birthday.

⌘⌘⌘

A few times in previous months Ursula and I, with my cousin Manfred and his wife Eva, had sat and discussed the economic conditions in Canada. We thought that for young people things were probably better there than in Germany.

So, on the spur of the moment and feeling very adventurous, the four of us drove to Bonn, where the Canadian Consulate was located, and applied for immigration visas.

To everyone's surprise, we received the answer a mere few weeks later that all four of us had been accepted.

We quit our jobs and packed our belongings, but kept our immigration plans secret until the last possible moment! When we finally told everybody, they were shocked.

To soften the impact a little, we said we were just going for a year or so to see how the other side of the world lives, to have a good time, and then we would come back. I don't know if anyone believed us.

We said goodbye to our families and friends and left Wuppertal on a train bound for Bremerhaven on the fourth day of October. We sailed from Bremerhaven on October 5, 1957, on the good ship "Seven Seas," destined for Montreal.

The Seven Seas was by no means a luxury liner. It had been an Allied Troup Carrier during the war and afterward was fitted to carry immigrants without many improvements to the cabins. There were still four bunk beds and metal lockers in every 10x10-foot cabin.

Needless to say, at check-in men and women were assigned separate cabins. Not what I had in mind for a voyage that might otherwise have served as our honeymoon.

Then, after a journey of a little over a week, we saw an extraordinary sight as we sailed past Halifax, Nova Scotia.

To this day I remember my first glimpse of the gorgeous fall colors to the left and the right as we sailed down the Saint Laurence River towards Quebec City.

I had never seen such brilliant colors. The deepest reds, the purple hues, orange colors with yellow tints, and some green speckles in between. I considered it an omen, a sign that our move to the New World would be good for Ursula and me. It looked to me like the rainbow at the end of the pot of gold. We disembarked in Montreal on the 16th day of October, with $102.00 to our name.

The first couple of weeks we stayed with my cousin Lothar, who in March of that year had followed his brother Wolfgang to Canada.

Wolfgang had been educated in hotel management in Switzerland and was now the headwaiter in the main dining room at the Queen Elizabeth Hotel in Montreal. Lothar had found a job cooking chocolate at the Cadbury factory.

By the middle of November we moved into our own furnished apartment on Dorchester Road. We had a living room and a bedroom, which we could lock. A community kitchen was in the middle serving four families, and a shared bath and toilet were down the hall.

Times were tough in Montreal. Unemployment had risen to above 15 % in the city during the fall of 1957. As hard as I tried, I could not get a decent job.

It did not help that the people in Montreal love to speak only French. As I found out, they hated the English language and spoke it only if someone forced them to!

At the public school in Lauscha I had received three years of English language education and I'd told Ursula that I could speak English well. I would understand everything and be able to converse with people, I'd told her, and she had nothing to worry about. Boy, were we in trouble!

So, I had no job and no prospects, I could not understand and converse with people, and unemployment insurance for newcomers was nonexistent at that time. Our money ran low fast.

Thank God, Ursula found work as a maid for a Jewish family who owned a shoe store downtown on Christina Street. She was to clean their home and look after their two small children on the other side of Mount Royal in the suburbs, while they were at work downtown at their store.

She had to use two different streetcars and one bus to get there, all without knowing the language. So Wolfgang made up sign cards indicating transfer points and her end station. She did very well getting around Montreal on her own, but we were always relieved when she showed up after work in the evenings.

But the financial reality was that the money she made was not enough to pay our rent and living expenses. So by early January of 1958, after less than three months in Montreal, Ursula and I scraped together the last of the money left over from our original nest egg, sold Ursula's prized umbrella for an additional $5.00, took some money that my cousin Manfred sent us, and bought two bus tickets to Sarnia, Ontario.

Manfred and his wife Eva had ended up there after parting company with us in Montreal, and he had found good work as an electrical motor-re-winder at Delta Electric.

Manfred wrote to say that it was probably much easier to find work in a smaller town than in a large one such as Montreal. That made sense to us, so we packed our belongings and made the 500-plus mile journey south to Sarnia in a Greyhound bus.

As we approached Sarnia I noticed a sign saying: "15 miles to Petrolia." The name brought a laugh out of me, as petroleum was a common name for lamp oil in Germany. I did not know that Petrolia had been the birthplace of oil exploration in North America.

Nor did I know that this obscure fact would soon have great significance for me, as the auto industry would shape my destiny – and I would have a role in shaping the destiny of that industry as well.

⌘⌘⌘

Ursula and I were flat broke when we arrived in Sarnia on the 10th of January 1958. We did not even have a dime to buy ourselves a cup of coffee.

Eva introduced us to Emma Hickey, a German lady who had come from Swabia ten years earlier and now worked as an assistant at the Sarnia Hospital, where Eva met her while giving birth to her twins, Monica and Marion.

Emma owned a house right next to the hospital, and, lucky for us, had an apartment for rent and a heart as big as her house.

Emma was the friendliest person and the kindest soul I have ever met. She rented her apartment to us without reservations. We had no money and no work. But she looked at us and said, "I trust you." She also started immediately to talk to people she knew to get work for us both.

She was successful. In just a few days, we were both working and earning.

She charged us $15.00 per week for the fully-furnished, 3-room apartment, all utilities included. But, secretly, she also gave Ursula $3.00 back each week, with the advice to save that money for herself and not to tell me. She said – and she believed – that a girl needed a little extra cash of her own. "For emergencies!" she told Ursula.

We lived with Emma on George Street for about a year until I found better, more suitable, work in Sombra, a very small town about 20 miles south, located directly on the St. Clair River.

I had been hired to maintain and repair the machinery at a paper-converting factory, making gummed packing paper and scotch tape, photo corners, and tarpaper for insulation and as a moisture barrier.

The owner's name was Bill Dahm. He was an Austrian citizen from Vienna and a very likable fellow. His whole family was in the paper-converting business; they had other factories in Austria, England, and Sweden.

During the War, Bill had fought on the German side and was captured in Italy in 1943 and sent to a prison camp near Kingsville in Ontario. He stayed in Canada after the war and decided to open a factory there.

Shortly after I started to work there their office assistant quit and I was able to convince Bill to hire Ursula to run the office. As an added bonus, we got to live on the beautiful Saint Clair River, and we made friends in Sombra who we still have to this day.

My mother visited us twice during this period, one time staying for more than three months. She liked the tranquility and beauty of the area and loved to sit by the river. She did the shopping for us at the local variety store, where you could buy everything from meat and sugar to horseshoe nails. She became friendly with the owner, Mr. Hargrove, after assuring him that she did not know, and had never met, Mr. Hitler.

I worked at the paper-converting factory through 1963.

Then the opportunity to buy the machine shop I mentioned earlier presented itself. I took it, and worked hard at it for a little over a year till I ran out of money.

And this is how I came to North American Plastic and the plastic parts supply business.

CHAPTER 4: North American Plastic

My training in Detroit concluded in June 1965, and I was ready to start the job in Wallaceburg. By that time the construction phase of the new North American Plastic (NAP) factory in Canada had concluded.

The new plant was 400,000 square feet, consisting of three big buildings. The center building housed the molding room, with its high bay and ceiling for two cranes and a balcony. We eventually filled it with 22 injection-molding machines ranging from 450 to 3000 tons.

To the left, looking from the front offices, was the decorating building with two flow coaters and three vacuum chambers for metallizing. On the balcony we had 10 paint booths, and in the front area was our laboratory.

Our very important paint storage and mixing room was built to be explosion-proof and was located at the rear of the building. A couple of years later we added a chrome-plating machine to the other half of that building.

To the right of the molding room was the assembly building, with three conveyor lines, our warehouse, and two shipping docks. Every area of the plant was well lit; there were windows everywhere. It was the most beautiful and the largest factory that, until then, I had ever seen.

During these early days I came home most evenings excited to tell Ursula about all the new and wonderful things I had seen and learned.

By July, the first six molding machines, ranging from 3000 tons to 450 tons, had been installed up at the plant in Wallaceburg. The decorating department had the coaters, the chambers and the paint booths installed and the overhead conveyor system was ready to take the first load of plastic parts. In theory, we were ready to roll!

However, what we had not yet done successfully was train our new work force.

Wallaceburg is a small town of about 12,000 people. They had never been exposed to a plastics manufacturing plant, never mind a quality plastic parts plant with the processes necessary to take plastic pellets and make shiny auto parts from them.

Expectations had run high in the town. Everybody had thought this would be easy money!

Expectations were even higher from our Big Three customers. We had promised them timely deliveries. Quotas had been set and deadlines were approaching fast. Parts needed to be shipped. These commitments had to be honored!

Our very first job at NAP was making armrests for the Ford Comet and Fairlane models.

But the workers were not ready! And this is when I was first introduced to the concept of Murphy's Law: "If things can go wrong, they will—and at the most inopportune time!"

The injection molding of the parts went OK, we had all the ABS (Acrylic, Butadiene, Styrene, a hard plastic) pellets we needed, and there were boxes full of molded armrests ready to be decorated. But the processing through the flow coaters proved more difficult than anticipated.

Somehow the viscosity of the base coat was not right, the temperatures not exactly right, the lacquer at first was too thick and then, after we over-corrected the problem, to thin. And then — was the speed right in the coater?

So, many of the initial parts ended up with runs on them, or a variety of beautiful rainbows. Unfortunately, both are undesirable features on armrests.

These were the first of our plastic parts to be introduced to landfills around the town of Wallaceburg! (The owners of these "landfills" were paid handsomely for the use of their property to dispose of our scrap parts.)

This went on until someone from the 10 Mile plant sent a grinder over and we learned we could grind up the scrap parts and send the reground material back to the 10 Mile plant for reprocessing.

As for the workers from Wallaceburg, we had seriously underestimated both the attention span of ordinary people struggling to acquire complicated skills.

There was a high degree of precision required to mix the lacquers and paints and set the correct operating speed of the machine for each process. The experts at the 10 Mile plant had been doing it for so many years they were able to do this in their sleep. Not so the new employees at the new plant.

Tempers ran high among us supervisors during those first weeks. We worked day and night to pass our knowledge on to the workers about how to duplicate the processes time after time. There were many nights I did not go home, but slept in the chair in my office for a few hours before going back to the shop floor to try to solve another problem.

The upside to these long hours working together to resolve problems was that we all became good and lifelong friends!

Thank God, the management people at DPM had had the foresight to only give us their backup set of tools for these early trials.

As a result they were able to help us out, so that we ultimately met our production quotas without jeopardizing quality during the first couple of months while we slowly ramped up production.

Eventually our Wallaceburg workers were trained, all positions got filled with now-qualified personal, and we began to run the plant like it had been intended to run.

We educated the new people in the proper ways of purchasing, scheduling, inventory control, molding, mixing solvents with paints, metallizing processes, and the additional decorative painting of automotive instrument clusters with the high quality our customers expected.

Some of our painters became so proficient that they were later asked to become trainers for the paint department at the DPM 10 Mile Road plant.

⌘⌘⌘

As for Ursula and me, finally we were doing well. We purchased our very first house.

It was a ranch house on Sandra Crescent in Wallaceburg, with an attached garage, a large living room, a kitchen, a laundry room, and three bedrooms: one for us, one for Andy, and one for Karin. We thought that we had made it and that we were rich now!

Never mind that we now had a mortgage, and a second mortgage privately arranged through our attorney. (I still think there was something fishy about that arrangement, the way he managed to get us that second mortgage from a farmer in Wallaceburg. Once a month I had to drive to this farm and deliver a check to him)! But we managed to pay off the second mortgage after two years.

At the time, somewhere around 1967, there were probably a little more than 25 pounds of plastic parts being used on a car; all still only interior trim parts, mostly decorative instrument clusters, parts on door panels, some heater ducts, and outlet parts, all small to medium sized.

However, I noticed that all these parts got a bit larger and a little more complicated every year. The choice of the molding materials at the time was ABS, or polypropylene.

In May of 1967, Bob got fired for having established a little private enterprise on the side, making structural spindles for our manufacturing process at NAP. That would have been OK, but using some of our employees to make these spindles on company time was not a good idea!

Mike's lawyers questioned us, the original five at DPM, but we knew nothing about the whole affair.

We later found out that Frank, the alcohol-loving scoundrel referenced earlier who had been hired earlier that year, was the one who had called Pete at the 10 Mile plant and reported the shadow operation. As a result, we got a new plant manager, one of many to come, hired by the Detroit staff.

The first one was Jim, who thought he was God's gift to women. He was an Italian-born stud and went after every female in our office and the plant. He lasted little more than a month! We saved him from serious injury by sending him back to Detroit before the male population of Wallaceburg, and the neighboring Walpole Island, an Indian reservation, had a chance to do him bodily harm or to scalp him. (We employed quite a few native Indian women at that factory over time.)

Our first real big job came the following year.

Andy, our Ford sales engineer, had managed to get the order for the 1968 Mustang console, and right after that, the contract for the 1969 Fairlane console.

These two consoles were the first of the bigger plastic parts that were to come during the next few years.

Ed was the buyer at Ford purchasing and (another) Ed was the engineering manager for both projects, with surrogates named Tom and Ian assisting him.

Another guy named Mike was the purchasing manager at Ford. He spent a lot of time with Mike Ladney at our plant during mold tryouts at the startup of production of these two consoles. He was an elderly cigar-smoking and tobacco-chewing man. He was ready to retire and he wanted to make sure that no blemish would come to his record before he did.

I got to know him well during that time and we had a number of lunches and dinners at the Wallaceburg Inn Hotel, where he stayed during the start-up phase.

Ursula did not appreciate my time at the hotel after work because it took time away from her and our two very young children, Andrew and Karin. I did not realize it then, but it was at this time that I started to spend more time at work than with my family.

The tools for both consoles had been finished at our Paragon Tools shop. Paragon was located in Windsor, Ontario.

Mike Ladney had purchased the tool shop in 1963 when he realized that owning a shop capable of making our own injection molds would give us a big cost and timing advantage over our competition. We started to mold these big consoles in beautiful colors, without paint!

These were extremely big pieces of ABS plastic running down the inside center of the car (It was the largest piece of plastic in a car at the time, and a first for us in the industry). It separated the two front seats and butted up to the rear bench seat.

Both consoles had been engineered to have a container for gloves and accessories with "spring-loaded coin slots" (This was also made of ABS plastic, and produced in-house at our 10 Mile Road plant).

The console was designed to be an integral part of the interior, and the center focus, of the car.

At the early design stage, the concept appeared impossible to achieve, but Hugh and his engineers at Paragon Tools designed and built the injection molds with a collapsible core system, which allowed such a complicated part for the first time ever to be de-molded.

(After filling the mold with plastic and forming the part, the core-half of the mold is manipulated through hydraulic pressure to become smaller, thereby allowing the part to be de-molded from the cavity side.) It was truly an innovation and, as I stated earlier, a first for us and for the plastics industry.

The Mustang console was finished with a camera-case grain and we molded it in five different colors.

The Fairlane console had a unique grain design that proved impossible to de-mold without grain damage. With the help of Ken at Ford's styling studio we were allowed to reduce the grain depth slightly, and that helped the consoles be molded without damage.

The console's glove box was also new. It was molded from polypropylene, with an integrated "living hinge" to replace the conventional metal hinge.

The added benefit was another reduction in weight and a considerable cost saving over a conventional "assembled-on" metal hinge.

This was another industry innovation for DPM back in 1968.

I was thinking about that living hinge the other day when I saw one advertised as a breakthrough patented invention on some plastic storage container, incorporating the lid. We could have done this over 50 years ago! We were just not focused on housewares at the time (and plastic containers were not exactly on every shelf either).

We flocked the glove box to give it a velvety touchy feeling and the glove box lid was made from our self-skinning polyurethane foam, which we produced at our 10 Mile Road plant.

With all these new "in house" capabilities, we at DPM stayed ahead of the competition and continued to grow. It was all about innovation and giving the customers more than the competition could offer.

By having a presence at our customers' purchasing, engineering, and styling departments to promote our capabilities every day of the week, DPM made a name for itself!

Naturally, we at NAP benefited from their success. We assembled all the parts, including the console mounting brackets (and the console light, which we purchased).

We shipped the finished assemblies to the Ford assembly plants in Dearborn, Michigan and Saint Louis, Missouri.

With the two consoles from NAP, and other plastic parts produced during that time by us and by our competitors, the industry added about 15 more pounds of plastic to cars. There were now close to 40 pounds of plastic on an average car, and the majority of it had been taken away from metal!

Plastic on automobiles was now on its way!

CHAPTER 5: Battling the Unions - 40 lbs.

At that time, circa 1968, plastic parts were still only used on the interior of the car, in decorative, non-functional applications.

But that year, something unexpected happened to us at NAP.

The Canadian United Automotive Workers (CAW) decided to call a strike at our plant.

We quickly found out that the strike was not about money. It was all about work rules. The CAW wanted to control what our workers in our plant could and could not do. In other words, the union wanted to take management control away. We had no intention of letting that happen.

The CAW had been established in Canada a year earlier to represent the workers at the auto companies in Canada

It was closely affiliated with the UAW in the U.S. North American Plastic was one of the first new supplier companies being located in Canada because of NAFTA.

The newly elected president of the CAW wanted to establish himself as a tough union man. Since NAP paid higher wages than any other company in Wallaceburg, the CAW president decided to strike over "skilled trade worker" (mechanics and electricians) rules. This, we could not agree with!

Wallaceburg, with a population of 12,000 people, quickly became a divided town. Families were torn and fought against each other. The men mostly wanted to strike. The women, liking the relatively easy work and the money it brought in, wanted to work. But the union won and the strike began.

It became ugly very fast. In order to supply parts to our customers, we had to hire "scabs" – temporary workers willing to cross the picket lines of striking workers.

We brought them into our plant with our own buses, which we had to purchase, picking them up at prearranged meeting places at the start of their shifts and taking them home at the end of the shift.

Anything to keep our production going!

We began to receive threats. The threats were made in person or by telephone, and our workers from Wallaceburg and the surrounding area became afraid. Every day fewer people showed up at the bus pick-up locations and we were starting to have problems maintaining production.

Then, something interesting happened that saved the day. One of our workers, an enterprising individual of Portuguese descent, saw an opportunity and came to our office with a plan! He said he could get good workers from Portugal to replace the strikers. We agreed to hire as many workers as he could bring to us.

Jose called a contact in Portugal and managed to get about 70 people on a couple of airplanes a few weeks later. They flew into Toronto and then on to Windsor where we picked them up and took them to Chatham. Immigration quickly cleared them and gave them temporary work permits. The Canadian government was very interested in bringing new people to Canada during the late '60s!

It was a win-win situation. Jose provided them with room and board, we had workers that we desperately needed, they had work, and Jose had another source of income.

The deal was that we gave the workers' paychecks to Jose and he would first deduct the monies for room, board, and their flights to Canada!

This arrangement, as strange as it sounds, was happily accepted by all of our new workers; and it lasted until the end of the strike. Jose asked every week if we needed more people because, he assured us, he had plenty more he could bring.

I have to add that these were really good workers and that we kept every one after the strike was settled. Almost all of them became Canadian citizens after the required five years of residence.

Jose became a wealthy man. He entered politics later and was very popular with the Portuguese-born population.

The strikers, for their part, were naturally furious. Things began to get dangerous.

They attacked the buses daily with rocks and stones and any other thing they could throw until the Ontario Provincial Police had to give the buses an escort to and from the plant.

A number of times strikers threw metal chains across the power lines to the plant, interrupting electrical power and shutting us, as well as parts of Wallaceburg, down for hours until Ontario Hydro could restore it.

A few times strikers threw eggs and other things at *my* house on Sandra Crescent, leaving me to clean our front windows and doors in the morning.

We finally had to put cameras on the roof of the plant, and were able to catch most of the culprits in the act and give the police the film for prosecution.

In the end we prevailed, and after two years of this madness, I believe that the CAW was told by the main United Auto Workers union management in Detroit to settle the strike, as it had become an embarrassment.

We always thought that it had been the ego of the President of the CWA at the time that created this problem, as he just wanted to make a name for himself.

The strike lasted two years and it has been a valuable lesson to me. Always fight with every ounce of strength for what you believe is right!

Eventually every lawsuit the CWA brought against our management team and NAP was dismissed at the Canadian High Court in Toronto.

I had the opportunity to attend some of the court proceedings to testify and found them very interesting. It amazed me to see and learn to what extent people will go, lying and perjuring themselves.

But, as an added bonus to me, I found Toronto nightlife a lot more lively, interesting, and entertaining compared to Wallaceburg, to say the least.

CHAPTER 6: Plastic Conquers the Interior

In the spring of 1969, on one of his European trips, Mike Ladney visited a tire manufacturer in England where he met Bill, a very talented time-study engineer.

Mike asked Bill to come to Canada to join our NAP team. In the summer Bill and his wife Shirley, and their sons Kevin and Martin showed up in Wallaceburg. Ursula and I showed them the area, helped with their search for a house, and from then on quickly became pretty good friends.

Bill contributed greatly to our manufacturing processes with his time studies. He made us more efficient, saving us money and ultimately making us more competitive – which led to more work placed at NAP by the auto companies.

He was also a very good entertainer. He played the piano and the guitar well, and we spent many evenings together with our growing families, singing, drinking beer and having fun.

Bill also introduced us to a new way of hiring office secretaries. After the applicant had answered all the relevant qualification questions, they were asked to walk straight toward a wall, hands by their sides; and if their shoes touched the wall first, we found an excuse not to hire them!

Looking back now, it is hard for me to believe that this really happened. But this is how it was back in 1968!

⌘⌘⌘

In the meantime, our salespeople had brought in orders from General Motors, Ford, and Chrysler for more ABS and polypropylene interior parts for our plant in Wallaceburg.

Plastics could now be found almost everywhere on the inside of automobile passenger compartments.

They appeared on the instrument panel; the A, B and C Posts (the A Posts are to the left and right side of the Windshield, the B Posts separate the front, and the rear doors and the C Posts are at the left and right side of the rear window), door and quarter panels, consoles, and at many other places previously occupied by other materials.

Just before the start of production on the consoles, I was asked to become the quality control manager.

With my engineering background, and the ability to read prints and interpret specifications, the Detroit management figured that I was the right person for the job. And I guess that by that time DPM management figured my English was good enough that I could be let loose on an unsuspecting customer's quality control department.

Needless to say, I accepted; and soon found myself traveling regularly between our plant in Wallaceburg, the Detroit plant, and our customers' facilities in the Detroit area.

I loved working with customers, especially with the various engineering departments. But the design, styling, quality, and even purchasing, processes were equally fascinating to me.

There was so much to learn. Purchasing wanted cost savings, engineering wanted weight and part consolidation savings, and design and styling were literally trying to study what could be done next!

So my education continued, and at a pretty good clip. I met on a regular basis with the GM, Chrysler, and Ford Motor design and styling engineers to discuss what was being worked on.

My role was to help them determine if a specific new project could be made with a plastic material and, if so, if our company could be the source for this new part.

As soon as I perceived the possibility of a new project, I contacted our sales engineers to swoop in and the opportunity further.

Another benefit to this role was that I had chances to visit the various assembly plants of our customers. This is when I could see if any of our competitors had problems with their parts. I visited assembly plants on a regular basis and called them my "good will trips." But while there I was spying on our competitors' product quality. I passed this intelligence on to our engineers.

I was fascinated by how these parts from all over the country were put together and, at the end of it, miraculously, a brand new finished automobile rolled off the assembly line.

Also, it was quite an education for me to see how the workers at the assembly plants interacted with their management. Right from the start, I could see that there was no love lost between the two factions.

Workers hated their jobs; they just liked their paycheck every Friday! I tried to understand how working eight hours doing the same boring manual work day after day could create resentments.

To emphasize this point, one day I was at the Clark Avenue Cadillac plant responding to a problem they had with installing the instrument panels we supplied.

The Clark plant was already a very old plant then. The car chassis started being put together up on the third floor, hanging on an overhead chain conveyor coming down to the lower floors while various parts where being assembled onto the chassis.

I was in the plant tending to my instrument cluster panel problem when all of a sudden I heard a commotion a floor up where the radiator was being installed. I was nosy and wanted to know what was going on so I went to investigate.

I saw to my surprise that the worker there was driving the attaching screw through a misplaced hole in the frame, right into the radiator – with the result that radiator fluid was rushing out onto the floor.

I could tell that this worker knew very well what was he was doing, but that he could hardly wait for the next chassis so that he could drive another screw into the next radiator. This went on for quite a while, and he enjoyed every minute of being in the limelight. His co-workers began to cheer him on.

Finally, a supervisor came, quickly assessed the situation, and shut down the conveyor to stop the madness.

On my next visit to the Clark plant, I asked what had happened after I left and found out that the supervisor in charge had been fired for not being there to shut the conveyor line down immediately.

The worker had not been reprimanded. He had been told to drive a screw into the hole, and that is what he did.

End of story!

Input from assembly line workers was neither wanted nor appreciated back then. The worker's job was to do as he was told! The workers' response to this job climate is what I had witnessed.

I observed a number of similar cases during my years at the various assembly lines and I saw no real behavioral difference at any of the automaker's plants. The attitude of all the autoworkers appeared to me to be the same, "I know that you are screwing me and I am here to put in my eight hours; but I will do as little work as I can get away with!"

On a sideline: I had the opportunity to visit the Henry Ford assembly line in Dearborn, Michigan in August of 2016 and I can only marvel at the technical advances that have been made since my time on the front lines.

These advances make the assembly line today much more "worker friendly" than those I observed at auto plants more than 35 years ago – and I am sure that, today, worker input is encouraged and appreciated.

⌘⌘⌘

Reducing the weight of cars had already become a technical and financial issue back in the late '60s and early '70s. (Fuel efficiency was not yet a big issue because gas was cheap. This changed after the first oil embargo in 1973!)

Plastics were being explored for use everywhere on the interior of the car. With a relatively low-cost tooling investment, with ABS or polypropylene parts could be molded out of plastic in every contour and shape. These were still the two main choices of materials to replace heavier metals. ABS was for harder structural parts, while polypropylene was for parts requiring a softer, warmer feel.

A, B and C posts that had up till then been made from metal were now being replaced with plastic, as were quarter panels, parts of door panels, glove box doors on the instrument panels, knee bolster panels, and steering shaft shrouds. There were opportunities everywhere. It was like Christmastime for the plastic parts supplier industry!

We at the DPM group made sure we got our share! At NAP we managed to get the quarter panels for the 1969 Ford Mustang and Granada models.

During the design phase our engineers suggested that we make a few changes to the mold, molding the fasteners right onto our panels, which would save more money. That suggestion was accepted and Ford engineering and purchasing staff were happy. We had scored another first!

Andrew and Karin were growing up well in the Wallaceburg area. I had put a swimming pool in the back of our house on Sandra Crescent. Andrew and Karin loved it and spent a lot of the summer in the pool with kids from the neighborhood.

That year my sister Barbara decided to follow me and emigrate from Germany. She arrived in Wallaceburg in 1969 with her newlywed husband, Horst. I managed to get her a job in our laboratory to get her started, and she did well working for our company.

I was spending a lot of time away from home, being sometimes at the plant at all hours of the night, or being at DPM in Detroit, or at our customers. But Ursula handled herself well, making new friends and bringing up our children.

Her closest friends were named Shirley and Theresa. We all spent a lot of our weekends together drinking Molson Canadian beer and, as I said earlier, singing songs. Occasionally Ursula and I would go to Sarnia on weekends to spend time with our closest German friends, Horst and Ursula (Doe), Heinz and Gisela, Wolfgang and Peggy, Manfred and Brigitte, all of whom we met when we first went to the Sarnia area.

And on Saturday evenings we went to the Polish Canadian club in Sarnia to dance and drink the night away. The only problem was the 30-mile drive back to Wallaceburg at 2:00 o'clock in the morning.

Thank God nothing bad happened during these late night drives along the St. Clair River, considering that we had sometimes consumed quite a number of beers!

Ursula was now over 21 years old and no longer had to hide in the bathroom every time a policeman or Salvation Officer came in. When we first came to the Sarnia area bars, or beer parlors as they are called in Canada, we could not tell the difference between their uniforms – and Ursula ended up hiding in the bathroom many times until the perceived danger had passed.

One of the big challenges with designing plastic parts for cars at that time was that there were no existing specifications to guide us.

The material for these new products was still largely an unknown to the automotive engineers. The plastic parts replaced mostly metals, rendering useless all previously known and established tests. What was also very important was that we were able to combine other parts or functions into our plastic parts, which previously could not have been done.

This posed enormous challenges for both our automotive customer and for us suppliers. Purchasing departments wanted the potential cost and weight savings to be projected in advance!

Interpreting the existing, mostly metal, specifications and correlating them to plastic on the quality control side was the hard part, then weighing the pros and cons against the cost savings or economic advantages on the purchasing side of the equation.

Thank God that the economic side won hands down most of the time so we had more and more new products and parts to produce.

But nobody could write new specifications and test procedures fast enough for these newly designed plastic parts.

However, economic conditions demanded that these parts be installed as fast as possible. That is why many of these newly-created and produced parts ended up on cars long before the tests were completed. Therefore, some of the new parts warped out of shape when the temperature climbed to 130 degrees inside the car in the summer's heat, and developed gaps and creaked when it fell below zero in winter.

But the engineers worked together day and night to solve these problems. A lot of friendships between customers and suppliers were formed during these days as everybody had a stake in the success of plastics.

CHAPTER 7: The Shrinking Supply Base

A brand new day had begun for the plastics supply base and many companies were jockeying for a position to be a part of it! So this was also the period during which the first real culling of plastic suppliers began.

Those unable to actively participate at the design stage and the engineering and trial phases were swiftly eliminated. These suppliers fell by the wayside, to be replaced by those who could supply the needed technical input and support.

Spending time at various customers' specifications departments was key to getting new or modified specs approved.

I freely admit now that I wrote, or rewrote, quite a few of these specs in our favor, sometimes in the middle of the night before the quality inspector arrived in the morning. Because without the proper applicable specifications, signed-off prints, and styling approval no ISIR (Initial Sample Inspection Report) would get an approval by the customers quality inspector.

Without a part approval we could not recover the money that we spent during the year or more of building the tooling. By the end stage that money was desperately needed. In the case of the console, the tooling cost we advanced approached $300,00.00.

This may seem like a lot of money, but I can assure you, years later I came back to our plant with checks of way over $1 million in reimbursed tooling costs.

For the car companies it was just as important that we were allowed to ship the new parts needed by the car assembly plants.

Most quality engineers that came to our plant to approve new parts were very thorough, detail oriented, and very fair quality engineers. But they also needed to learn with us about these new plastic parts' performance!

None of the plastic parts made during that time were vital load-bearing, safety-related, or exterior parts. They were eye pleasing, decorative interior parts only.

⌘⌘⌘⌘

Accuracy in color matching was another big challenge in the early days. Previously, all parts inside the car except vinyl or leather seats had been painted. Paint was easily matched and the parts next to each other would look the same.

Now we introduced pre-colored ABS and/or polypropylene to the existing vinyl to save on painting costs. But we found that every raw plastic material supplier used a different method to achieve color matching.

To make matters worse, the various styling departments created different types of grains for the parts, such as Corinthian or Mediterranean or Camera Case, just to mention a few. All grains reflect light differently, and to make matters more difficult the colors would look different on the same grain if it was on an ABS versus a polypropylene part.

Furthermore, as everyone sees colors differently, it was very difficult for us to get new colors approved on a new part. And ABS parts generally appear shinier than parts molded from polypropylene.

What did not help was that the styling engineers approved raw material suppliers based on color matches on plaques made under laboratory conditions.

Then later, when we molded our production parts, the color appeared different on a contoured part, producing a noticeable color variation.

Sometimes, there was no way that a mismatched molded part could be installed in the car, and we ended up painting the parts anyway to achieve the desired color.

With ABS parts, that was not a problem, the paint adhered; but with polypropylene material, because of its higher oily-wax content, saturation was more difficult and the parts needed a special, mostly flame, pretreatment before painting -- and that was very costly.

Naturally, with this option came the question of which party would pay for the extra paint operation. As always, everyone looked for somebody else to blame for any failure. However, in all the times I was involved in the color approval process, the molder was never found guilty because we had to buy the "approved material from an approved source."

Eventually, these problems were resolved, the offending colors were fine-tuned by the resin manufacturer, and the painting stopped.

But, in those early days, the same problem would be repeated the following year.

Despite the challenges, NAP became a very successful company producing consoles and interior parts. During the late 60s and throughout the 70s we molded and built plastic parts for the Fairlane, the Mustang, the Versailles, the Thunderbird, and the Diamond Jubilee for Ford; the Pontiac, the Cadillac, the Chevrolet and the Buick for GM; and the Barracuda and Sebring for Chrysler.

⌘⌘⌘

The early 70s brought the large station wagons, and with them another considerable jump in the amount of plastic material – and with it came more challenges!

I remember vividly the three Ford station wagon panels that we had been awarded.

The left-side plastic panel of the cargo area was six feet long, over two feet high, and with a five-inch horizontal ledge to butt up against the car's rear window. At the time it was the largest panel ever designed in plastic to be fitted into a car.

The right side had been designed in two pieces: the one closest to the rear seat was mounted stationary, and the other one by the back door was removable to allow access to the spare tire.

We had no problems with the two parts on the right side, but the left side gave us a number of sleepless nights. After it was molded, it ended up being too long by over an inch.

For some reason the checking fixture to check the contour and dimensions of the part had not been completed, probably because of the numerous engineering changes that had been made during construction of the injection mold which had been done at our Paragon Tools plant in Windsor Ontario.

I remember having to drive the finished parts to the Ford pilot plant on Oakwood and I-94, in Dearborn, Michigan, where all new parts got installed into simulated assembly line conditions to check their viability and how they are best added to the assembly line flow.

There I was, as proud as a peacock, bringing these monstrous parts to the pilot plant. I had rented a truck in Wallaceburg the evening before to hold a dozen of these huge panels.

As requested, I got there by 8:00 a.m. sharp, unloaded my precious cargo, and met the plant and design engineers. Everybody looked at the panels in awe as we walked to the staging area. Then we tried to install them into the rear of the station wagon.

But as hard as we tried we could not fit the left panel into the cargo area, even using a two-by-four and a crow bar. The part was too long to fit into the space it was designed for.

Ford Purchasing, Engineering, QC, and all the Pilot plant people were present as well as Hugh, our mold-building genius. Almost immediately the finger started pointing at us. We did not use the right mold shrinkage for such a large panel in polypropylene – that was the first accusation thrown out by the body engineers.

"Yes, we did use the right shrinkage," was Hugh's answer. But since the checking fixture was not present, we could not prove our case; and time, as always, was running out on us.

Since the chief engineer had certified this chassis body as correct, the decision was made to use this particular station wagon body as our new master gauge. Prints were redrawn right there at the plant and the mold was shipped back to Paragon Tools to be changed.

What made matters worse was that, in order to save mold construction time, the mold had already been grained; so any changes to the visible surface meant it would have to be re-grained by hand.

But the changes to the mold were made in record time and the newly molded parts fit like a glove to the station wagon body.

By then the checking fixture was available and we saw to no one's surprise that the newly molded parts did not fit the fixture. We found out a week later that Ford's chassis engineering department had, without notifying anybody, made a change to the body to reduce the cargo area by — guess how much — an inch!

The mystery was solved! We were innocent and Ford purchasing had to pay us for all the changes and overtime incurred.

With those types of engineering changes, we managed to get a little extra money, which we could always use!

But, what was more important, we got the production parts to the assembly plant on time for the launch of the new Ford station wagon. Again, we had saved the day and were the heroes at Purchasing.

As an interesting little sideline: these three plastic panels had been designed to snap onto metal rails that secured them to the cargo floor. It had been my responsibility to find a suitable, qualified manufacturer to supply those rails.

I found a fledgling metal "bender" company (metal-bending) providing metal parts to the auto industry in the Toronto area. It was run by a man named Frank Stronach and four other Austrian/German immigrants, and was called Magna Co. They did an excellent job and we bought these rails from them for the next five years.

Little did we know that over the next fifty years Magna would grow into one of the largest and one of the few surviving plastics and all-around parts suppliers to the auto industry worldwide.

By the time we started to produce the plastic station wagon panels in the early seventies, the average car used more than 50 pounds of plastic.

But still, almost all the plastic was used only on the interior of the car.

But now another development was taking place at the auto companies.

Management at the Big Three were pushing to further reduce the plastic parts supply base in order to reduce the workload of their purchasing and engineering staffs. There were just too many plastic parts suppliers competing for the same business.

Because DPM, North American Plastic, and Production Molded Plastic (Mike had recently purchased this molding plant in Akron, Ohio) were able to produce these and similar parts with our big molding machines, had our own Paragon Tool shop, and had other production plants and a top-notch engineering staff, we remained solidly on the ever-shorter supplier list.

However, some of our closest and previously fiercest competitors were starting to be eliminated.

CHAPTER 8: Chrome on Plastics - 50 lbs.

During the late sixties, it became apparent to Bill Best that the auto engineers and stylists wanted to add more chrome parts to the exterior, but without adding more weight to the car.

DPM and plastic were ready for the task!

Bill convinced Mike Ladney to get into the chrome-plating-on-plastic business and found a company making plating machines! Mike took a group of us to Brooklyn where the company was located. We stayed in a hotel in Manhattan and took the New York City subway to the shop.

The machine was a special chrome-plating-on-plastic machine complete with a pre-plater (a completely new science), which was capable of leapfrogging parts from one tank during the plating process over to others, already in use. It was supposed to save plating time.

But the machine we bought, (it was the only one they ever made,) turned out, as Mike said many times, to be made by Rube Goldberg.

It was far more complicated than any one of us had anticipated. It looked good in theory but was just bad in practice!

At the time the machine was priced in excess of two million dollars. Needless to say, with all the trouble we had getting it to function as intended, they received considerably less! As a matter of fact, the company declared bankruptcy the following year.

The pre-plating process involved a series of tanks with a number of different chemicals prepping the ABS plastic mechanically through etching, to be made conductive with a copper solution in order to accept the electrolytic copper-nickel-chrome deposits. (Again, a completely new science.)

Without going into too many details, like removing the Butadiene from the Acrylamide, or counting the many sleepless nights we spent with that machine, plating on plastic in the seventies was a new, completely unproven, process!

We burned through three "expert plating managers" in less than a year, and had countless chemical engineers spending day and night at our plant trying to solve one problem after another.

All we did during the first year of operating the machine was produce tons and tons of partially-plated scrap plastic parts. Some looked like copper, some like nickel, some like chrome, and some had a little bit of all of them. At that time, we did not yet know how to separate the metals from the plastic to recover the plastic for regrinding.

Thank God we found plenty of farmers in the area willing to take all that scrap to be buried on their land – for a lot of Canadian dollars, of course. I often thought at the time, "What will people in the future think when someone digs there and discovers all these buried bits of shiny multicolored plastic?"

But eventually, after considerable time and energy spent—and I think I noticed my first grey hairs around that time—we managed to get the process under control.

And out came shiny, completely chrome-plated plastic parts that looked just like heavy metal parts, but were considerably lighter in weight – and they ended up costing a lot less than their metal brothers or sisters! Equally important was that they passed all the required tests! The plated-on metals stuck to the plastic!

The first real production order we received for this process was for the Chrysler Barracuda rear reflector grilles. It received a lot of attention from the automotive engineers and was written up in all the plastics magazines.

After that success story we at NAP received some orders for front grilles and headlamp bezels from General Motors for Chevrolet models at their Flint, Michigan plant.

Unfortunately, Chevrolet insisted on molding the grilles at their molding plant in Flint, I believe to satisfy their union. The parts were shipped to us for plating with the finished parts to be returned to Flint for assembly onto the car.

This was definitely a bad idea! We found out the hard way that the molding and plating of parts belong together.

The molded parts need to be plated right away in order to detect if any stress problems had occurred, before molding thousands of parts that cannot be plated successfully.

Predictably, we ended up producing a lot of badly plated grilles, which created a problem between our respective quality control departments.

It took me a long time to convince Flint that the scrap grilles, after we had unsuccessfully plated them, were definitely their responsibility.

⌘⌘⌘

Shortly after we started the Chevrolet grille program, we had visitors from Volvo in Sweden.

The Volvo director of purchasing, three engineers, and two lab technicians spent a week with us at NAP and with our Paragon Tools engineers. As the saying goes, "It was the start of a beautiful friendship."

They liked what they were seeing and the way we operated the plant and handled our daily business!

After they returned to Sweden, we received a request to bid. We sharpened our pencils and shortly thereafter received the orders for the 1972 grilles and headlamp bezels for every model from Volvo Co. in Sweden. NAP continued to supply Volvo grilles and headlamp bezels every year from then until 1988.

NAP was now in the international automotive business!

North American Plastic shipped three or more containers of chrome-plated grilles every week to Sweden—including the diagonal strip with the black Volvo emblem and the two headlamp bezels. Every part was molded, chrome plated, and painted by us in Wallaceburg!

All the industry's automotive engineers began designing their new grilles and headlamp bezels to be chrome-plated plastic. The weight savings allowed the auto companies to put "shine" back on the exterior of their vehicles.

Plastic was finally conquering the exterior of the car, and it inspired engineers to conceive and design more and more plastic parts for use on the outside of the automobile. Door handles and bezels and fender or door side strip moldings were designed in chrome-plated plastic.

Previous attempts had been made to mold bumper fasciae or covers on some low-volume models, with some success; and I will write about that a little later.

I must say that working with the people of Volvo was the best experience I had with the automotive companies.

As a supplier to Volvo, you were always treated with the utmost respect at purchasing and engineering, styling, the laboratory, and at every other place inside the Volvo factory.

They listened to and worked with us to avoid potential problems, and never quarreled about money or asked us to reduce our prices. Requests for price reductions had become a regular demand from the North American auto companies and it placed serious financial pressures on plastic parts suppliers.

Volvo's personnel people, on the other hand, could not do enough for us. They would pick us up at the Goteborg airport, provide suitable lodging, and after all our meetings were finished, would take us back to the airport.

But they also appreciated the duty-free liquor that we brought with us, as the alcohol at their local state-controlled store was very expensive.

(A bottle of scotch retailed for over $80.00 at that time, if I remember correctly). But I considered that a small price to pay for all their kindness and fair play.

I took Ursula with me a number of times
and she loved being shown around the town of
Goteborg and having lunch with some of the
wives of my purchasing or engineering contacts.
We had many dinners and good times with all of
them in the evenings. We were even invited to
their homes and we spent a few weekends at
their cottages with them.

⌘⌘⌘

It is during this period that I became a
regular international traveler. I began travelling
to Europe on a regular basis and Mike had
drilled into me that "You can't sell from an
empty wagon!" Therefore, every time I traveled
to Europe, I took some of our nicely plated and
painted sample parts with me.

When I got to Germany, I used my
mother's basement cellar in Wuppertal as a
storage place. (Thank God she no longer needed
the space to store coal for the winter!)

Over time I had quite a number of parts
stashed over there and I showed them to
European automotive manufacturers as well as
potential joint venture partners.

One of our partners was Peguform in Boetzingen, Germany, a large plastic injection molder who, under our license, began to make polypropylene fascia assemblies for European car companies. They also licensed a paint-solvent recovery system for their paint department, which Bill had developed for us at DPM.

During that time, Bill and his team also developed what we called "idiot lights." It was a system on instrument panels whereby the instructional messages are completely hidden until they are illuminated, and become visible only when the panel is backlit. That was another industry first, invented and developed for us at DPM.

In 1972 we also managed to get the order to convert the Volkswagen Beetle "die-cast" headlamp cover to a chrome-plated plastic part – only as a service replacement part to start, but it was a way to get onto the VW's supply base and become an "approved supplier."

Back home in America, all the Big Three auto companies liked those shiny plastic grilles and headlamp bezels with their associated weight and cost savings.

And they liked chrome strips along the side of the cars, and taillight assemblies; so our plating on plastic business picked up rapidly.

Mike Ladney saw the growth in this part of the business and acquired two more, financially struggling, plating companies, which we converted to plating on plastic.

The first one was Production Plated Plastic near Kalamazoo, Michigan and the second was Universal Plated Plastic near Fort Wayne, Indiana. Overnight we became the largest producer of chrome-plated plastic grilles, headlamp bezels, and other plated-plastic parts in North America, if not worldwide!

By then I had been promoted to corporate quality control manager for the entire DPM group, now consisting of 6 separate companies, on top of my duties in international sales and joint venture business development in Europe.

But I never, ever felt overworked. I never even considered that what I was doing was real work! It felt more like a grand adventure because every morning brought something that was new and exciting to me!

I constantly met new people, engineers, purchasing agents, or officials from other plastics companies.

My corporate quality control manager position became a "last resort" position only. Every one of our plants had its own QC manager quite capable of handling its daily affairs.

I was only called to represent a corporate or management position to the customer in cases of a major quality dispute.

DPM had six plastic manufacturing plants with over one million square feet of manufacturing space and the largest mold-building facility now — and Mike Ladney solely owned all of them.

CHAPTER 9: DPM's Acquisition Phase

One morning Mike asked me to relocate my office from Wallaceburg to the 10 Mile DPM plant. That did not come as a complete surprise as some of my automotive purchasing contacts had mentioned this before. Of course, I agreed.

My friends at NAP did not like that I was moving away, but they all wished me well and gave me a big party, and I promised to stay in touch and keep an eye on them.

I had trained and promoted a woman named Odessa Patterson to quality control manager and she took my leaving her, as she called it "to hold the bag," specially hard.

Ursula and I packed up all our belongings again (this time it was considerably more than two suitcases) and moved with our two children to New Baltimore, Michigan on Lake Saint Clair.

Initially Ursula wanted no part of moving to "Detroit."

In Wallaceburg we received much bad news via TV and radio out of the Detroit area, mostly connected to the Detroit riots of 1967.

It took quite a bit of convincing to persuade her that the New Baltimore area, 25 miles to the northeast of Detroit, would be a very safe place to bring up our children.

And so we left on the 15th day of October 1972, exactly 15 years after coming to Canada – and I do mean exactly to the day!

We moved via the ferry in Sombra/Marine City to the United States.

My mother had been with us that summer, and she liked the new house that we purchased in New Baltimore, with the big garden and the swimming pool.

So there I was, 15 years older — then 36 years old — and again in a new country. At least the language was the same! Or was it?

Andrew was 8 years old and Karin 6. They started school in New Baltimore and were teased quite a bit about their Canadian "eh" language skills, and also the way they were dressed.

Andrew shrugged it off, but Karin suffered, and after two days came home from school with hives all over her body, which the school nurses misdiagnosed as measles.

But after a while both children settled in, and each found new friends and began to enjoy their new surroundings close to Lake St Clair.

Ursula and I joined the New Baltimore Newcomers Club and made new friends too. They were all our age, with similar interests. Most of the men were working for the auto industry in various capacities and most of the women were stay at home moms. Unfortunately, my social life came up a bit short during this time because I was away so often.

My international duties kept me many days and weeks away from home and family, especially during the summer and fall days when new car models were being built at the assembly plants and introduced in showrooms.

By now, almost all of the "visible" interior parts of the cars were made from some type of plastic materials.

Around 1973, in addition to our regular business, which had grown to over $100 million annually, DPM became deeply involved with plastic bumper systems development. With this development, we were getting into real safety issues, like the 5-mile-an-hour crash tests.

Our engineers, with Bill Best, had approached the safety issue by backfilling the glass-filled polypropylene injection molded bumper-shell with a closed-cell polyurethane foam to absorb the energy released in a front- or rear-impact or crash.

That meant many hours trying out new polyurethane mixture formulas and then trips from our laboratory to the customer's lab to get our system tested by the auto company.

We finally managed after many tries to receive the required approval!

There it was: a 12-pound plastic bumper beam with some modern technologies could outperform a 70-pound old-fashioned steel bumper! Plus, it would never rust and was installed at a considerable cost savings to boot!

That was yet another first for us!

And what was equally important, it kept us on the "favored supplier" list, which continued to shrink.

The car companies were really working hard to reduce their supply base and a lot of attention was given to the capabilities of a supplier's technical engineering department.

Purchasing people from all three companies had come up with new requirements that a plastic supplier had to spend at least 5% of their annual revenue on research & development. (When you have over $100 million in sales that adds up to a lot of money!) And every year we had to prove that we were making that R&D investment again!

By then, all of the plastics knowledge resided with the suppliers, and the car companies realized that they had no choice but to rely on our expertise. And the better we (at DPM) were able to represent ourselves, the more new jobs came our way!

By 1975 there was already close to 150 pounds of plastics used on cars; but there were a lot more opportunities on the horizon.

Around March 1975 Ursula's sister [in Germany] wrote to us that she and her husband Lothar, along with their children Dirk and Anja, would like to visit us later in the year, and that they wanted see a little of the United States. That news created quite a bit of stress in my work life and at home. They intended to stay with us for five weeks!

I knew I could not spend that much time with them, but I wanted to show them as much as possible and give them a good time.

I borrowed Bill's 30-foot motor home, and on the 29th of June we all drove from Michigan to the airport in Newark, New Jersey to pick them up. Remember, at that time, you were still able to get right to the plane.

Here they came, all four of them in blue jean suits coming down the stairs of the plane like movie stars. It was a stunning site that I will never forget.

From Newark we drove north to Salem, Massachusetts, where the Parker Brothers toy and game company is located.

We had invented a foam football a few years earlier and were producing the Nerf balls at our DPM plant for Parker Brothers.

I had pre-arranged a meeting for our little tour group with Mr. Parker, the owner and he greeted us in his office. I think he was over 90 years old by then.

The Nerf footballs as well as the Ack-Ack guns that shoot Ping-Pong balls, both of which were manufactured by us, made Andrew and Karen very popular children around the New Baltimore area, as we had plenty of them around the house for them and their playmates.

Mr. Parker had his assistant show us around the three-story factory with its heavy wooden floors, where we got to see all the old and new Parker Brothers games. He gave Lothar a German-language Monopoly game. He also provided us with a guide to show us around Salem and explain the somewhat notorious history of the town, known primarily for the hunting down and burning of witches a couple of hundred years earlier.

The next day we drove up the coast to Maine, stopping a few times to swim in the Atlantic Ocean. Lothar had both a video camera and a regular camera and he took pictures at every opportunity. As a matter of fact he drove me nuts, asking me to stop at every corner so he could take a picture or a video.

Sadly, on one occasion he left his camera on a rock while we all enjoyed a swim in the ocean. A few hours later the rock had been covered by the waves and the camera, with all those pictures, was gone forever. He never got over that (and he tried to put the blame on everybody except himself).

While on the East Coast we devoured I don't know how many pounds of fresh fish, lobsters, and clams, and enjoyed them immensely.

We then drove across New York State to Niagara Falls, spent a day visiting the spectacle there, and then through Ontario down to Sarnia, then across the bridge back to our home in New Baltimore.

After the two weeks away from DPM (no cell phones yet!), I think I spent the next week working 14 hours a day trying to catch up on things I had missed – and just maybe to get away from Lothar for a few hours.

It was 1975 when we got involved with plastic wheel covers. Mike had met Ed, an engineer and inventor, at an auction where Ed was trying to find a buyer for his invention of a spring steel wire system that fitted into the groove on the rim of the steel wheels.

Mike saw the opportunity and the potential. If this wire could be attached to a plastic cover, it would make for a revolutionary new lightweight wheel cover assembly.

Mike authorized Paragon Tools to build a prototype plastic wheel cover mold, and we started to mold lots of plastic covers. We decorated them and attached the wires to them and I went with a stack of these prototype covers to Ford Motor Co. to get them into the system for an approval.

Larry was the engineering manager of the wheel cover department, and Bill and another Larry were his foot soldiers.

I wined and dined this group, including taking them to the Indianapolis 500 and to a lot of Wolverine football games in Ann Arbor for over two years. (Mike was a University of Michigan alumnus, and he had 10 seats on row 35 right on the 50-yard line).

In this new market, we were now competing with already established metal wheel-cover suppliers.

During this time I learned the extent to which an established company with resources will go to prevent a new competitor from entering a lucrative market.

Mike told me many times to: "Don't be discouraged! Fight for it! Remember, there are four of these things going on every car."

I did as I was told. But I forget how many times I heard that one of our covers had failed or "fallen off." But no one could say exactly why, because the failed covers could not be found, were broken, or were "lost in transit" on their way from the test track in Romeo, some 40 miles to the north! Because of that, we had to start new again.

Finally, we had enough. I took 30 of our prototype plastic wheel cover assemblies to Mercedes in Stuttgart, Germany and requested that they test them at their track.

I received a positive response after several weeks that our covers had passed with flying colors and that they liked our system. Some weeks later their engineers designed a new plastic Mercedes cover with our spring-wire system. We found a company in Germany to mold and make the covers there under our license.

With the approval and success story at Mercedes in hand, I went back to Ford again with the solid cost and weight savings advantage and, with that, was finally able to overcome the obstacles. But it took a long time!

I am convinced that without the Mercedes success, the special interest group of people would have kept the door shut against us much longer! But in the end we got the contract for the Ford Fairlane and the Ford Taurus wheel cover assemblies.

DPM received a good price for the covers we shipped and it was considerably less than the cost of a similar metal cover – and our plastic part weighed less. It was a win-win situation!

DPM had produced over 12 million of these plastic wheel cover assemblies until the time I left the company in 1986.

By the late 1970s close to 180 pounds of plastic was used on a car. And still there were many more opportunities.

What a way to go! We obviously could not be involved in every new development, but we were still on top of the shrinking supplier list.

During 1979, Chrysler was not doing well and needed a new vehicle success story – something revolutionary and eye-catching, but relatively cost effective to build. After many different studies, their choice was to bring back an improved version of the minivan.

What was of extreme interest to us, and to our competitors, was the interior trim panels Chrysler intended to use.

They wanted to use polypropylene, from the instrument panel all around to the rear cargo door. And the Chrysler engineers had decided to use only one manufacturing source for all of it, to eliminate the constant problem of color mismatch! As a matter of fact, they demanded that all parts used on the vehicle be molded from the same batch of material and coded as such!

We and four other companies were invited to participate in the bidding process and, if I remember right, we gave a number of capability presentations to their engineers. Hugh and his team convinced Chrysler that we were up to the challenge.

After many meetings at the Chrysler head office in Detroit and at our plant, Mike received the call from Chrysler's purchasing agent that we had been awarded the program.

We found out a few weeks later that behind the scenes Mike had made a side deal with Chrysler: all of a sudden we were the proud owners of the Chrysler plastic-molding facility in Michigan City. Coincidence? I do not think so.

We now owned nine plastic-producing plants in the U.S. and Canada!

I remember driving to the plant with Mike, Bill, Hugh, and Rudy after the Michigan City deal was made public, for an official welcoming ceremony. There we all got a glimpse of Mike's personality, as it was evolving.

We stopped near Kalamazoo at a restaurant called the "Steak and Ale." Mike had a few martinis and ordered a pound of Alaskan crab legs.

He loudly questioned the weight of the order, making a scene. He asked the waiter to bring a scale to prove that the portion served to him was a pound. The waiter did so, and showed Mike that the portion was in fact more than a pound.

Mike laughed the whole thing off as a joke, but the rest of us were embarrassed. He had become so sure of himself that he thought he could now do anything he wanted. I did not know it then, but this time possibly signaled the start of DPM's decline.

Later, on the final leg to Michigan City, Mike boasted about how great things were going for DPM and how we were all going to be millionaires.

I am here to say that proved to be false – as far as everyone but Mike was concerned!

⌘⌘⌘

Late in 1983, the first "minivan" in the U.S. rolled off the Chrysler assembly line. I believe that model saved Chrysler, and it boosted the DPM group to the top of the heap – we were the biggest plastics company in North America.

DPM became the proud owner of one of the first new Chrysler minivans that rolled off the assembly line! It had close to 40 pounds of plastic added to the interior of the car!

DPM got involved in a couple of other programs during the early 1980s.

General Motor engineers wanted a complete plastic inner door panel assembly for their Beretta model, with the glass, the window lifter mechanism assembly, the locks, seals, wiring, and speaker attached. The prototype program was awarded to General Electric, who attempted to mold the panel in a glass-filled sheet-molding compound.

It was doable and worked, but the part weighed over 40 pounds, with the cure (or cycle time) over 10 minutes per part. That combination of factors was unacceptable to the GM engineers and their cost analysts.

GM Purchasing approached DPM, and Mike authorized Hugh at Paragon Tools to build a mold, at our expense. We molded prototype door panels with Mike's patented gas-assist system, where all heavy sections of the panel were hollow-molded, resulting in a much lighter, but still strong, part.

Our part weighed 17 pounds and the cycle time was 3-1/2 minutes per part. (More about gas-assist on the next pages.)

What a success story for DPM, being the innovators of yet another new processing technology!

I have more to tell about this particular program a bit later because after I left DPM, I worked on this panel at Voplex.

Unfortunately for all of us, the Japanese car companies entered into the U.S. market just at that time, and their success forced GM to cancel this particular model for lack of sales.

⌘⌘⌘

Mike had gotten interested in gas-assisted molding back in 1977.

It had been patented by Jim Hendry, an American residing in England, and was being used in Europe on molded parts through Cinpress, a British company, under a limited license from Hendry. On one of his trips to England Mike met Hendry and persuaded him to sell the rights to the patent.

Mike had quickly seen the advantage of the weight and cycle time savings process and, after he brought it to us at DPM, we used it successfully in our plants wherever feasible; giving us additional cost advantages over our competitors.

I particularly remember one story. Mike had bought four plastic chair molds at an auction and he told Hugh to switch to the gas-assist system for this production. Shortly thereafter we secured a contract to mold chairs for K Mart.

It should have been a roaring success. However, in order to improve the profit margins Rudy had used a higher than recommended percentage of reground polypropylene material.

The result was that our very first shipment of chairs—five railcars' worth—was rejected. (The fact that Rudy kept his job indicated to us that Mike had been somehow involved in the debacle.)

That project was never revived, and we ended up with a whole lot more waste white reground polypropylene.

Again we learned that innovation carries its risks.

⌘⌘⌘

To that point, in the early- to mid-80s, the magazines that covered the plastics industry ran almost weekly advertisements for auctions of plastics machinery and tools. Those machines were from competitors that had to declare bankruptcy and close their doors. But that is how we were able to update or add to our molding capacity during these years!

Around 1980 Mike bought an old plant on 15 Mile Road just west of Van Dyke Road. It was a sprawling factory complex where the Briggs Company once made bathtubs, sinks, and other similar products. The plant was far too big for our use at the time, but Mike wanted it.

The advantage was that it had enough floor space and ceiling height to contain five or six 3000-ton, three 1500-ton, and six1200-ton injection-molding machines.

Mike could see that interior automotive plastic parts were getting larger – but more importantly, that on some models exterior parts such as bumpers, fenders and hoods were also being designed with plastic in mind. Mike wanted DPM to be ready for that.

The plant was so huge that I almost got lost trying to find my office the first time. My office was in the front, on the ground floor next to a showroom big enough that I could display samples of all our best products! I had a corner office looking out to 15-Mile Road. Mike had long wanted a plant with a rail siding for shipping and receiving, which this plant had.

And he also had another plan. To our surprise and delight, Mike had half the side parking lot torn out and replaced with a Japanese garden.

This garden featured a little creek running through it with a couple of wooden bridges, a large pond with Coy carp, and fountains comprised of bamboo buckets that tipped with overflowing water.

He imported Japanese cherry trees and placed benches underneath them. Japanese music played at all times!

This was different! It was an incredible Asian wonderland right outside our executive dining room facing 15-Mile Road. Our garden was an exact duplicate of one we had seen while visiting one of our licensees in Tokyo.

⌘⌘⌘

Gas-assist molding was here to stay. Weight had become an increasing issue for the automakers because of new government regulations targeting automotive fuel standards. All car companies wanted the weight and cost advantages gained from gas-assist molding. That promised to be good for DPM. Mike now owned the worldwide patents for it.

But Mike unfortunately tried too vigorously to control many bidding processes for new jobs. He wanted to cash in on this in a big way and his aggressiveness created many difficult situations for me and for DPM.

On one hand, the car companies wanted the savings associated with gas-assist molding; but on the other hand, they could not award every job to DPM.

However, Mike demanded a royalty from anyone molding parts that used the technology.

His royalty demands obviously made the parts more expensive and therefore diminished their attractiveness. Many senior automotive executives and long-time friends met with Mike to try to work out compromises. Mike maintained a stubborn refusal.

As a result, in the early1980's they began referring to Mike as "the mad Russian," as in "The mad Russian is at it again." (Mike's parents had emigrated from Russia.) Far too often, jobs ended up being molded the old fashioned way because the car company would not submit to Mike's blackmail.

CHAPTER 10: The Europe Strategy Matures - 200 lbs.

But while we faced these new domestic challenges the "DPM Group" had become a global player, supplying chrome-plated parts directly to European automotive customers, and indirectly through joint ventures or licenses with European and Japanese parts suppliers.

Our first joint venture had started in 1965 with VDO of Germany, which licensed a number of interior painting and decorating technologies from us, and later our solvent recovery technology which was used in all our painting facilities.

In 1972 we joint-ventured with Peguform, another major European plastics company, which licensed molding and painting technology for bumpers; and later licensed the foam-filling bumper technology from us.

Since I spoke German, Mike "reassigned" me to help develop these and other potential German opportunities.

Peguform was located near Freiburg in southern Germany, a beautiful city with a walled-in, inner old town. A man named Erhard was the CEO and another named Uwe was the chief engineer, with a gentleman named Frey assisting.

Whenever I visited I stayed at a fashionable, first-class hotel called the Hotel Colombia. It had a very cozy bar, and in the evenings after dinner I stopped by for a nightcap.

The bartender was from Spain and he was an expert on classical music. He favored tenors, and I told him that I liked Luciano Pavarotti. He said he knew someone who could sing even better than Pavarotti, and it was he who introduced me to the voice of Placido Domingo. After a long day at the plant, I enjoyed many evenings at that bar, discussing classical music, sipping cognac, and listening to classical opera arias.

Many years later, when I was working for Cambridge, I visited Freiburg with Ursula and we stayed at the Hotel Colombia; but the Spaniard, I was told, had retired and gone home to Spain.

Another of our joint venture partners was the Brose Company in Coburg, Germany. Under our license they produced the Volvo "see through" foamed headrest.

Bill Best and his crew had made the prototypes, using our own "closed cell, in-the-mold painted self-skinning" urethane foam developed at our Detroit plant.

But Volvo calculated that the freight and logistics costs from Detroit would be too high and suggested that we meet with the Brose Company to work out a licensing deal.

I visited Brose at their plant in Coburg many times to check on the quality of the headrests during start-up and the early production phase, and I always found the quality to be excellent.

There was a personal bonus for me as during this period I was able to visit Lauscha in Thuringia where, as mentioned earlier, I had spent 10 years of my youth.

Lauscha was only about 35 miles to the North, but it was still on the other side of the Iron Curtain at that time.

However, I never had any problems crossing the border, as I had become an American citizen in 1977 after passing the U.S. five-year residency requirement.

I drove the short distance and enjoyed many hours with old friends, discussing our school years and other local stories.

We made absolutely sure not to let the talk drift towards politics, never knowing who might be secretly working for the East German police and spying on our conversations! That put a necessary limitation on many discussions, but seeing them again was a delight nevertheless.

Between my regular duties as head of quality for (at that time) eight separate companies, I was deeply involved with our European plastic joint-venture partners, licensees, and their respective customers. I was also still responsible for the Volvo account, since quality and engineering go hand in hand.

Therefore, I spent a lot more of my time away from home, and in meetings with customers and our European partners – in conference rooms or at airports, hotel rooms, and restaurants.

It was during this period of dynamic industry development that the thought of writing a book first entered my head. The environment in which plastics took over metal in cars would be a story worth telling, and I had intimate knowledge of it.

Many times as I was racing from a 2 ½ hour 10 a.m. meeting at the tech center on Van Dyke at 12 Mile Road in Warren all the way to a 1 p.m. meeting at purchasing on Rotunda in Dearborn, I would have only enough lunchtime to grab a take-out sandwich to eat in the car.

I figured I'd probably have to name the book "Tennis Shoes and Corned Beef Sandwiches."

I was away so much that my daughter Karin wrote in a school essay in her senior year, "I grew up without a father." And at one of the school functions a teacher asked Ursula when she had lost me!

I also gained quite a bit of weight during this period, which, unfortunately, I still carry around with me to this day.

I thanked God secretly that I did not speak Japanese, where we also licensed DPM technology, so I escaped being sent on constant trips to the Far East. Goodness knows what that would have done to my waistline!

At one time my brother-in-law, Lothar, quipped that the doorknob to his house never cooled down because I visited them so often. But we all enjoyed the time together in Wuppertal, especially being with my mother and my sister Brigitte, both of whom I loved dearly. (My father had died in 1967 of a stomach problem brought on by taking an excessive amount of heart medication over the years.)

I did enjoy my frequent travel to Germany that allowed me to visit my family on a regular basis, and at no cost to me.

With just a little additional money I could take Ursula and the children with me whenever school time allowed it. And taking the family did not cost DPM because on most of these trips we stayed with my mother or with Ursula's family, and not in hotels.

However, there was one little strangeness about these trips. Whenever Ursula went with me we would end up sitting separately.

Since I usually traveled business class, I'd give her my seat, and she would sit in the front, getting all the attention and goodies while I sat in the back with Andy and Karin. But that was OK. Having my family with me made these trips the best.

My mother died in 1982 of cancer at only 67 years old. She was laid to rest next to my father at our family plot in Wuppertal-Sonborn, where my grandparents are also buried.

As I started to understand the differences between the ways purchasing and engineering departments in Europe functioned and our ways of doing business in the U.S., I tried to use it to our advantage.

We were developing a spoiler for a new Ford Mustang here in Detroit.

We had designed it by using two injection-molded shells, an upper and a lower, which we had foam-filled and glued together using the foam as a bonding agent.

At the same time, Ford of Europe was developing a similar sporty car, I think it was called the Panther, which also had a spoiler designed on the trunk.

However, their spoiler vibrated during test-drives and they were unable to eliminate the vibration.

I had been asked by our Ford purchasing agent to fly to England with our spoiler system and help their engineers review, evaluate, and test ours to see if it could be used on their Panther.

Mike and I talked it over and we thought it was a good opportunity for DPM and one of our European partners.

Therefore, I got onto a Northwest Airlines plane in Detroit with my spoiler at 5:00 o'clock in the afternoon, and made it through customs at London's Heathrow airport at around 6:00 a.m. the following morning.

There, I rented a car, put this monstrosity in the middle between the seats and drove off, never having driven a stick shift car in England.

I was sitting on the right hand side of a car in a bucket seat. All was well until I got to the first roundabout. Then disaster struck.

I was driving (to my way of thinking) on the wrong side of the road, holding on to the spoiler with one hand and having to shift gears with the other while pushing the clutch with my foot, or did I hit the brake?

I drove around that roundabout I don't know how many times, until I was soaking with perspiration. I knew I could not stay in there forever, so I finally closed my eyes and darted into the outer lane – with horns blasting all around me.

Miraculously, I arrived on time for the 10:00 o'clock meeting. I was to meet with the English, and also five German Ford engineers who had just arrived from Cologne.

This was to be one of the most bizarre engineering meetings I ever attended!

The first hour and a half was consumed with discussions about how many bottles of booze and cartons of cigarettes had been ordered at the previous meeting, and what was owed to the Germans who had bought them duty free and brought them to the meeting. Then the money had to be exchanged and nobody had change in the correct currencies.

It was painful for me to watch, but it got even more bizarre. The farce continued as the Germans then started to put in their orders for the English engineers to bring to the following week's meeting in Cologne.

Eventually I got really pissed off and was not at my best when I voiced my displeasure at what felt to me like their utter disrespect.

I was sweaty, frustrated, and exhausted, having spent all night on a plane, then enduring the stress of driving for a couple of hours on the wrong side of the road – and arriving on time – just to sit around listening to them discuss booze, cigarettes, and Deutsche Marks and pound sterling exchanges.

I had expected the European engineers to drool over our invention to stabilize the spoiler at high speeds.

But none of that happened!

It finally dawned on me that they hated the idea that engineers from the U.S. had found a solution to their problem. I happened to be the messenger, and they did their best to ignore me.

At around noon one of the engineers told someone to take our spoiler into the basement for testing, and I was told to go and get some sleep. They gave me the address of a hotel nearby and then went on with their regular scheduled business.

They were thumbing their noses at our North American interference, and they thought of it as interference. So much for international cooperation at that time!

As a final indignity, there was a fire alarm reported at the hotel where they had put me that night, forcing all the guests to flee outside in the middle of the night in their pajamas. No fire was found and I always suspected that the Ford engineers had somehow instigated the false alarm, to have some fun and get even with the American!

But the experience taught me another valuable lesson: never interfere in another business unless you have a solid plan — and the power — to take that business over!

While back in Dearborn our glued-together foam filled plastic spoiler for the Mustang became another success story, I believe that in England it was never brought out of the engineering basement.

Their Panther sports car was built without a spoiler.

⌘⌘⌘

It was during that period in the early eighties that I had to give up my corporate quality control position.

Plastic had become a "load bearing" material and we were so closely involved in the development of these parts that I was forever called to be in some other country and increasingly unavailable to represent the DPM Corporation at quality meetings. Our customers eventually demanded that some permanent person, stationed in Detroit, be available to them when needed.

I was really torn, because I liked being corporate quality control manager, taking part in the development and ultimate approvals of new materials. I liked the tryouts, including the failures; learning from them, and then being part of the ultimate successes. That position had really given me a bird's eye view of all the car companies' intentions for future plastic usage on their upcoming cars and models.

But on the other hand I also liked being connected with sales to customers and partners in the U.S. and Europe, and sales eventually won.

Mike was a very persuasive person. It was probably at a dinner at Carl's Chop House in Detroit that he talked me into becoming DPM's corporate sales manager.

This is where we had dinner many times with customers and cut many important deals (and where after dinner we always collected steak bones from the other diners for Mike's white German shepherd, Heidi.)

Andy Fulton, DPM's Ford representative, had left us a few months earlier for what he said were greener pastures.

"You might as well be sales manager for the DPM Group," Mike said. "You know all the buyers and engineers of all the car companies anyway!"

So, without any fanfare I was suddenly in charge of domestic and international sales. (Somehow, I don't remember a raise with this; but to be honest, Mike paid and treated me well.)

On the domestic side, I had to manage Jim, Sr. and Jim, Jr. of Chrysler sales, Bob at Chevrolet, Gene and Earl at Oldsmobile, Roy at Buick, and Dan at GM of Canada.

By 1983, DPM was the largest privately-owned plastics company in the world, with annual sales of close to $250 million.

We were producing and supplying both interior and exterior parts to all the domestic car companies (the Big Three), as well as to Volvo and Volkswagen.

We had licensing agreements and joint ventures going with the Japanese and other European car companies. In addition, Mike collected royalties from three German and two Japanese suppliers. And Mercedes paid him for the use of his patented gas-assist process in Germany.

We made highly decorative interior parts: A, B, and C pillar posts, door and quarter panels, armrests, consoles, instrument panels, package shelves, and head rests. We started to make small under-the-hood functional parts, and exterior shock-absorbing front and rear bumpers. And we also made fascias and wheel covers as well as chrome-plated and painted grilles and headlamp bezels.

By now, the U.S. plastic supplier base – ever smaller in number – was producing over 200 pounds of plastic parts for a car.

At a little bit over15 million cars built annually, the plastic giants like GE, Dow Chemical, Exxon, Eastman, DuPont and Shulman were all doing very well and were extremely appreciative of U.S. molders using their plastic pellets.

⌘⌘⌘

A little later, GE developed a new material specially made for wheel covers, called Xenoy. This new material mimicked nylon.

As was the usual practice at the time, GE's sales force "sold" the virtues of new materials to the auto company's engineers.

In this particular case, they had approached Ford engineers working on the Taurus program. This wheel cover, as designed, looked quite a bit like the Mercedes cover, which was molded in a PA nylon, for which DPM had received our first wheel-cover system approval.

Anyway, I was successful in getting the order for the Taurus wheel cover. The mold had been made. We started to mold. And then trouble started.

This high-strength material would not flow and fill the cavity without flow lines or weak spots in the molded part!

We tried and tried without positive results. GE made changes to the material and we tried molding again. Same problem! It took almost 5 months, with GE making numerous changes, before we were finally able to mold good wheel covers.

Ford ended up having to postpone introducing this type of wheel cover on their Taurus. GE tried to blame us for the failures. We in turn blamed GE. Mike finally filed a lawsuit. In the end GE settled and we were paid for all the time and effort spent trying to mold an untried and unsuitable material for this application.

What was really interesting to me was that GE's "good will" method of paying us was to supply material to us free of charge until the debt had been paid off.

Back in the mid- to late-70s, my main activity had been at Ford purchasing on Rotunda Drive and Ford engineering at the tech center on Oakwood.

Guys named Tom, Sandy, Don and John were my main purchasing contacts, with Al being their senior, and Jack the purchasing agent for interior parts.

Dennis was the buyer for our wheel covers; Dick was his senior, with Hugh as the purchasing agent. I knew all the engineering and styling group people associated with purchasing well. And I can say this with pride: I had excellent relationships with all of them.

However, I did have a problem with the luncheon habits of a few that I regularly associated and worked with.

Lunch started at 11:30 and there were at times 50 or more cars waiting to pick up the purchasing, engineering, and styling personnel and drive them to various eating establishments – the kinds of places where reservations were required.

Steaks, prime rib, lobster, fish, shrimp – everything was available, every day. (I entertained one person who, on a regular basis, ordered a couple of uncooked steaks to take home with him after our luncheon!)

And with lunch came the drinking! Silver Bullets, Rob Roys, Manhattans, whiskeys – neat, Whiskey Sours, gin and tonics, and vodka (served in water glasses).

The waiters at all the restaurants knew each person – and their choice of food and drink! In some places the drinks were already lined up at the bar before we got there (to save time for more drinks, of course!)

And please understand that this was all at our – the suppliers' – expense!

To be fair, I have to say that most of my contacts behaved admirably and I got most of them back to work on time, and sober, after lunch.

Lunch was supposed to be over by 12:30; but for some, it lasted until 1:30 – and sometimes until 2:00 o'clock! It should be quite obvious that in many cases, not much business got done in the afternoon.

This went on five days a week, every week until Christmas – at which time it got worse, because some of them did not go back to work after lunch at all.

This behavior was by no means limited to Ford Motor Co. The same culture prevailed at GM. The restaurants around the Tech Center in Warren, Michigan had their tables booked a week in advance, year in and year out; and the Chrysler people filled Joe Muir's Seafood restaurant and all the other fancy downtown eating establishments every single day.

Personally, I was also having a problem with this system.

First, there was no way we could do reasonable business with some of these people after lunch. Secondly, when I finally got back to the office, Mike would want to know where the hell I had been. And thirdly was my expense report, which Mike had to approve. (Of course he always did – recognizing that this was a cost of doing business, and that all our competitors were doing it too!).

But the worst part was my expanding waistline! Having a big lunch almost every day, and then having to sit down to dinner with Ursula and the children when I finally made it home, was taking its toll!

Thank God the car company executives finally put an end to this.

New rules were issued mandating that suppliers and contractors could only take members of their staffs out to lunch four times a year – and the value of that "gift" could not exceed $25 dollars at a time.

⌘⌘⌘

During the late 70s, Ursula and I started to get closer to Mike Ladney and his family.

Mike owned a "cottage" at the Horton Bay Club, by Charlevoix, where the company entertained important customers during the year, but especially during the summer and fall months. Mike kept a 26-foot motorboat there, and we spent many weekends with the Ladneys and our customers' families.

We would drive the motorhome from Detroit and head up north to have a good time. We all enjoyed the beauty of the area, the plentiful food and drink, and taking the boat out to Round Lake and then on to Lake Michigan.

Sometimes we had a barbecue in the evening (Mike loved to cook lamb shish kebob), or dinner at the Weathervane restaurant overlooking the lakes.

(We were all too aware of the fact that the customers we entertained that weekend would probably be similarly entertained by our competitors during the following weekends.)

On one Sunday morning we walked up to the Horton Bay General Store where I learned from the owner that Ernest Hemingway often stayed there, eating, swimming, and fishing with friends. He even got married in Horton Bay, in 1921. Hemingway wrote "Up in Michigan," "The End of Something," and "The Three Day Blow" while at Horton Bay.

I remember one special weekend we had some of our licensee friends with us from Germany. Mike had someone bring the boat down to the Detroit Boat Club, located at the end of Vernier Road on Lake Saint Clair. He boarded with our customers in Grosse Pointe, and headed for Charlevoix via the Saint Clair River to Lake Huron and then Lake Michigan.

Ursula, Andy, Karin, and I – along with Marguerite Ladney and their four children (Douglas, Jane, Carol-Ann and Nick) – drove north in the motorhome.

Mike had had the boat polished for hours before setting out – but astonishingly, somebody failed to check the engine oil.

Halfway up Lake Huron, just past the Saginaw Bay, the boat's motor quit with lots of smoke. They could not get it running again. The radio did not work, and no flares were on board. They had to spend the night on the dark boat in the middle of the lake.

They were finally rescued and brought to shore by the Coast Guard the next afternoon. I drove the motorhome over to pick them up and get them to the cottage.

Needless to say there was not a happy camper among the lot, including Mike, who was looking hard to blame someone. The Germans all grumbled: "All the windows on the boat were spotlessly clean and the brass highly polished, but the engine burned up because there was no oil; there was no navigation system; the radio did not work; and there were no flares or life preservers on the boat. We'll never do this again."

The Germans mumbled all this to me in German, and Mike kept asking me what they were saying. I did not have the heart to tell him.

And I heard that story retold many times by my German friends during the following years; in fact, whenever I met with them.

Andrew and Karin, Ursula and I enjoyed the times up north much more when we were not entertaining. Mike had given me the key to the cottage and permission to use it any time. He started to travel and be away from Detroit more often in the early 80s. These are the years we really had fun!

Needless to say, we made use of the cottage as often as possible, spending time around the beautiful Horton Bay area and enjoying the boat for just the four of us. In the fall, on the creek running through the property we watched salmon by the thousands swim upstream to spawn. What a sight!

And at the end of the season, it was my job to take the boat out of the water and take it into storage for the winter.

In 1982 Ursula and I were to celebrate our 25ᵗʰ anniversary. I thought long about how to celebrate this milestone in our lives.

During the development of the Ford Fairlane wheel cover program I needed a metal bender to manufacture the stainless steel rim and center hub required for our wheel cover.

After a considerable elimination process I'd selected a Detroit supplier named Fritz to produce the parts for us.

As we worked to develop the two stainless steel parts, he and I got close, and I learned that he owned a condo on 7 Mile Beach on Cayman Island.

I asked him to rent the place to me for two weeks and he agreed.

Ursula and I invited our long-time friends Horst and Do to come with us. We enjoyed each others' company, swam every day to our hearts delight, and had fun catching spiny lobsters and conch to supplement our diet. We rented a couple of scooters to get around the island and to the store for food and "greenies" (that's Heineken beer in Cayman Island lingo!) We had a wonderful time there at 7 Mile Beach.

The only hitch was that Ursula injured her back on the fifth day of our stay. Horst and Ursula had been designated to go to the store for more supplies. Ursula got on her scooter, and messed up her back trying to start it.

After that she could not move without great pain. We got her to a doctor who told us all she needed was rest, so we took her back to the apartment and put her into a lounge chair in the shade of a palm tree on the beach.

The rest of us kept swimming and snorkeling. We had found a really cool place to snorkel right behind an old cemetery (it was one of those with the big cement crypts visible from the road), about half a mile from the condo, near a turtle farm. There were lots and lots of beautiful coral in the azure blue ocean with thousands of multicolored fishes swimming around and through them.

And then there were those five-foot long barracudas swimming in the water right next to us. They followed us everywhere, never moving a fin, and never threatening, but being right there with us, watching us as we swam around.

Poor Ursula, still in a lot of pain, sadly missed most of this; and the flight home was a torture for her. (Back in New Baltimore the next day, she went to our chiropractor and he had her back to her normal active self in a couple of weeks.),

The vacation was an adventure I will never ever forget and was over far too soon. Except for Ursula's mishap, it was an absolutely beautiful 25th wedding anniversary trip for the two of us.

And Fritz never allowed me to pay a dime for the use of his beautiful place on the water. He told me over and over again that when he and his family were not using it, it was always available to his friends. What a wonderful gift!

CHAPTER 11: The Death Knell for DPM

Early in 1984, Mike called us in to the executive dining room for an important meeting. He brought Barry Driggers, his lawyer, to the meeting. Barry announced that Mike had been having heart pain the previous few months and that his cardiologist from Grosse Point had recommended he undergo a heart bypass operation. Mike had selected the Cleveland Clinic for the procedure, and was scheduled to go there the following week. In his absence Barry would be the go-to person.

Bill was to run the day-to-day affairs of the company, Rudy would be in charge of the actual running of the plants, Hugh would be in charge of all tooling and would run Paragon, and I would be responsible for corporate sales. We all agreed to it and wished Mike a speedy recovery.

Mike's operation was successful and a couple of weeks later Barry informed us that he was recovering nicely.

Please remember that in 1984 a heart bypass was still a rare and dangerous operation and the success rate was less than 50 percent.

Mike made it through the recovery period at the hospital and moved for an additional rest period to Port Royal, near Naples, Florida, where he had purchased a house in a gated community on the Gulf of Mexico.

Of note is that Mike and Marguerite's marriage had suffered during the previous couple of years. The bone of contention was that Jane, their oldest daughter, had met a dark-complexioned man, Hermes, a native of Brazil, while attending the University of Michigan in Ann Arbor. They had fallen in love and wanted to marry. But Mike put up many arguments and forbade the marriage. Jane married Hermes anyway.

Mike did not attend the wedding and he called his new son-in-law "nothing but an opportunistic black guy" (I am being very kind with my wording here!), who only wanted Jane's money and a legal way to get into the U.S.

Nothing could have been further from the truth.

Hermes was at that time already a high-ranking executive of the Bank of Brazil and, having been sent to U. of M. in Ann Arbor by his employers to learn the American way of business, he was doing quite well on his own.

We tried to tell this to Mike, but he would not listen. As they say, "Don't confuse me with the facts; my mind is made up."

In any case, Marguerite, his wife, stuck by Jane and Hermes, and from then on a rift started to form between them. Mike stayed away more often, and he was seen a number of times at Brownies on the Lake at 9 Mile and Jefferson, dancing with a brunette woman.

A couple of times when he and I returned from a European business trip together he asked me not to tell anyone at the office that he had come back with me. Soon, Mike and Marguerite communicated only when necessary and only for the sake of the business.

During the first month of his recovery, Mike stayed in touch through Barry Driggers who, besides being his lawyer, had become his friend and confidant.

Barry told us early in 1985 that he had convinced Mike to remain in Florida and let us run DPM the way it had been set up before the operation. That was good news to all of us.

Unfortunately, it did not happen that way. About a month later, Mike started to call us at 8:00 o'clock every morning from Florida, wanting to know what was going on. He demanded to know what everyone was doing, and tried to be involved in every detail and decision that had to be made.

This became a nightmare.

Whatever we did was second-guessed, or just arbitrarily overturned or reversed by Mike, which made it impossible for us to operate our $250 million corporation successfully.

This was especially true for me in sales. No matter what I did, it was wrong. I was too soft on our sales people. All our prices were too low; I needed to get price increases from our customers. And why were we not getting more business from the Japanese car companies. That is what I heard almost every morning.

It became almost impossible to get new contracts and, in some instances, because Mike insisted on raising prices on existing contracts, our reputation slowly started to nose dive. We started to lose work to competitors.

Mike came back from Florida in the fall of 1985, blaming all of us for the problems the company was having and, from that time on, started to destroy DPM with the same energy and vigor that he had used all those years to build it.

He arrogantly believed that DPM was too big to be ignored and that we (he) could do anything we wanted. I did not know it at the time, but he was the poster child for the phrase "too big to fail."

He told me almost daily in his office, "They need us! We are the biggest; we have all the technologies; and without us they can't build their cars." That was the illusion Mike was under and that was all he talked about.

All the car company executives who had been long-time loyal friends of ours, tried to reason with him.

They warned him that there were now serious competitors to DPM, companies that also had all the necessary equipment and technologies. They even tried to make compromises; but no matter what they offered, it was never enough for Mike.

And this is how the downward spiral for DPM started to accelerate.

Around January of 1986 I had started to sleep badly I developed breathing problems and started to have chest pains.

My doctor – I also used Dr. Perry at the time – sent me to the U. of M. Hospital in Ann Arbor, where I was diagnosed with coronary artery disease caused by stress. On the 15th of January I had my first angioplasty, with Ursula by my hospital bed.

After they removed the heart scope, I remember bleeding uncontrollably for a few minutes at my groin – until they put a 50-pound sand bag on the incision. How technology and medicine have changed since then! (Just think: that procedure thirty years ago was in its infancy, and now it is performed thousands of times a day!)

It was right then and there, as I was recovering, that I knew I needed to leave DPM if I wanted to be alive to reach retirement age.

There were other changes around this time. Our son Andrew, after graduating from Anchor Bay High School, had gone to Michigan State to study mathematics.

During his second semester he had been recruited by the Army and entered a basic training program in Georgia. After training he would be deployed to Fairbanks, Alaska.

Andrew did not want to go to Alaska by himself, so he convinced Lois, his high school sweetheart, to get married; and in May of 1985 they married in New Baltimore.

Ursula put herself in charge of organizing the wedding. The ceremonies were to be held in two churches. The first part was in our Lutheran church, downtown on 23 Mile Road; and right after we walked over to Lois's church, St. Mary's, and participated in a Catholic ceremony.

After a short honeymoon, the young people took their belongings and drove to Fairbanks, where he started his new Army job.

The following June, Ursula visited Andy and Lois in Fairbanks. She flew to Fairbanks via Seattle, and the three of them went on a camping trip into the Alaskan wilderness.

Ursula afterwards told me the story many times about seeing eagles catching big fish in the river just off the campsite, and elk or moose urinating right next to their tents, and having to hang all the food in a bag from a tree so the bears could not get to it. She also told me how cold the nights in the tent were.

I, for my part, used Ursula's absence to deliberate, compose, and hand in my resignation to Mike.

Mike was genuinely shocked when I told him I was leaving. It was the morning of June 6, 1986.

He had no idea why I wanted to leave, and did not want to hear from me how bad things had become, or how bleak I felt the future seemed for the DPM Group. He tried very hard for more than an hour to talk me into staying.

He reminded me of the good times we'd had during the previous 20 years, and noted our accomplishments and our ascent as a major global plastics supplier to the auto industry.

But when I tried to tell him that his attitude was destroying what we had built together, he could not hear any of that.

I had made up my mind that my health was more important to me than Mike Ladney or his company. I just could not handle the constant conflict between our customers and Mike, with his demons, any more!

During my 21 years at DPM I had received some earned-out stock certificates, which I told Mike I wanted to cash in. He wrote a check, right then and there, cashing me out without a word.

And so, we shook hands and parted company that same day, late in the morning.

When Ursula returned from Alaska I told her that I wanted to take a few days off, and that I had rented a cottage at Flowerpot Island at Georgian Bay north of Tobermory in Lake Huron.

Ursula, Karin, and I drove up to Port Huron and across the river into Ontario and up the peninsula and then took the ferry to the island.

Later that evening by the campfire and over a glass of wine, I finally told Ursula that I had handed in my resignation.

She was stunned, to say the least.

But she understood, and agreed that my health was more important than DPM. (And she also liked Don, who would be my future boss, whom she had previously met at social functions.)

We enjoyed a very relaxed and peaceful week at the island.

I never actually spoke to Mike again after that day. He wrote a couple of times from Florida some years later, inviting me and Ursula to come down and see him. I wrote back that we had schedule conflicts.

Marguerite had started divorce proceedings against him in 1988 and, in order to settle the divorce, DPM's assets had to be sold in bankruptcy court. Chuck Becker of the Becker Group ended up buying the assets.

I have never understood why DPM declared bankruptcy. The by-then massive company should have had enough real assets to satisfy any divorce settlement.

God knows there had been enough offers to purchase or partner with DPM from European and Japanese manufacturers trying to get a foothold in the U.S. market.

It was a sad and unnecessary end to a great company.

I can't help feeling that with the right people at the helm, the disaster could have easily been avoided!

CHAPTER 12: Stacking Plastics at Voplex

And thus began the second part of my adventure with loading plastics into automobiles!

Having decided to leave DPM, I had been in contact with a few of my friends at competing companies. One of them was Don Smart, the vice president of sales at Voplex Corporation. Don asked me to join Voplex. After many meetings, he made a favorable offer and I agreed.

Don had a very talented engineer named Joe as director of engineering, with Uwe as his assistant. Two gentlemen named Ken and CJ were our sales engineers at Chevrolet; John was the sales engineer at Ford; and Dennis was the contact at Oldsmobile and Buick with Griff supporting him.

Albert, who had officially retired when he was in his seventies, worked for Don on special projects. He was another talented engineer who had received many patents while working at Fischer Guide and later at GM.

And I was now working with these great people.

Voplex was smaller than DPM. The headquarters was located in Rochester, New York, and its sales office in Troy, Michigan. A grandson of the founder was in charge of the company.

Voplex was listed on the New York Stock Exchange and had two manufacturing plants in Lapeer and Vassar, Michigan, and one in Canandaigua, New York.

Don also had a sales agreement with JP Emco in Ada, Oklahoma, where their main business was making bumper fascias and bumper reinforcements for Ford Motor, and door and quarter panels for Buick and Oldsmobile.

Two people owned JP Emco. Pat was the manufacturing lead and Hugh was the CFO (but was somehow always absent whenever I was visiting their plant). A guy named Jim, who reported to Don Smart, handled their sales.

Don brought me on as marketing director, with a pretty good salary. Our offices were located at 550 Stephenson Highway between 14 and 15 Mile Roads, along the west side of I-75 in Troy.

And as a bonus, he had confided to me, they were about to sign a joint venture with a German company to build an extrusion plant in Canada.

That of course got me really interested, and was more or less the reason why I chose to join Voplex. I was hooked, and started to work for them on June 16, 1986.

The joint venture was with Happich, a company located in Wuppertal – my hometown!

I had visited Happich many years earlier with Mike. We were trying to negotiate a licensing agreement with Otto Happich's father, the owner at that time. That deal did not materialize, in my opinion, because of two elderly gentlemen who were both too set in their stubborn ways.

But, there I was in Wuppertal again.

Don, executive VP and my boss, Dick our VP of technologies, and myself were on the Voplex side; with Otto, the younger Happich — now the owner — Hans, the general manager, and Dr. Berg the CFO on the Happich side.

Voplex Happich Corporation (VHC), the joint venture, was going to produce extruded vinyl body side moldings for the North American auto market and the factory was going to be in Woodstock, Ontario.

Voplex was to be the operating arm of the joint venture, and Happich would supply the technical know-how and purchase all of the required equipment.

The first job VHC received was producing six different sizes of body side moldings for the 1988 Chrysler Le Baron.

The moldings were to be extruded in color, with a stainless steel stiffening stabilizer and two gummed, two-sided tape attached and, after that, end caps injection-molded right onto the extruded body.

That was pretty neat stuff. At least it was to me!

Happich had made all the tools in Wuppertal, tried them out, got the required sample approvals, and transported the tools to Canada. There they set up the twin screw extruders — German made of course — and after that hopped on a plane back to Germany, wishing us good luck!

Well… deja vu in spades! Whatever can go wrong must and will go wrong, at the most inopportune times!

Without going into details, the colors were not right, the twin screws screwed us, and the German guy, another Hans that Happich had send over to represent their side, was a real piece of work – in other words, useless.

He was a pipe-smoking, puffed-up guy with a Napoleon complex, but thank God he stayed out of our way. His only interest was that his exotic black wood furniture set got to Woodstock and into his office without any damage. He was on the phone all day long, calling Germany or the freight company, wanting an update on his furniture delivery.

Somehow I inherited the whole start-up of the job, probably because I spoke both English and German, and it was left to me to clean up the mess created by the Germans' hasty departure.

The Chrysler buyer was a guy named Don. Dave and Dwayne were the engineers responsible for styling and color and appearance approval, with Steve, the purchasing manager

(It was rumored that he was the half brother of the singer Madonna, but since he never got us any tickets to her shows we never believed it.)

Again, we were saved by a second set of tools that were operating in Wuppertal.

However, the airfreight costs from Germany were killing all potential friendships!

The people from Happich blamed " those stupid Americans and Canadians," and we blamed the typically over-engineered systems of everything the Germans had sent to Woodstock.

I spent over a month shuttling between Woodstock, the Chrysler factory, and our vinyl supplier trying to sort things out. Until, one day, everything finally came together; the people were trained, and our material supplier had fine-tuned the vinyl to be utilized in the twin-screw extruders (a process wholly new to them).

That was my first adventure at Voplex – and another one was just around the corner.

Don had succeeded in getting the contract for the complete— and I mean complete— interior trim system for the 1987 GM Beretta.

It included the A posts, door panels, quarter panels, package shelf, rear seat bench with storage boxes, and the instrument cluster with glove box and lid.

It was basically a 360-degree interior trim job, all with good old plastic materials.

In order to pull off the engineering, Voplex had hired an engineering studio in London, England, which worked wonders for us.

We received instructions or changes during the day from the tech center at GM in Warren and wired them to London in the afternoon; and they incorporated the new data or changes to the print, wired them back to us during the night, and we took them back to the tech center in the morning.

Our engineering world had truly become a 24-hour international wonder!

The green (environmental) movement in Europe was more advanced than ours in the U.S., and interior materials were starting to be engineered away from plastic.

A German company, Lignotock, had been successfully promoting a resin-filled (plastic) wood fiber — a renewable material — for door- and quarter-panels for the European car market.

We negotiated an agreement with them to license this technology for use on the Beretta program at our Canandagua plant. It is a relatively simple process:

A loosely non-woven wood fiber mat is saturated with just enough polyester to bind, and is compression molded with a low-cost mold into the desired shape.

Bingo! Out comes a panel to be covered with a decorative cloth, vinyl, or leather material.

The end result is a very strong and relatively light-weight trim panel, which gives it a cost and weight savings advantage over the typical injection-molded polypropylene panels then used here in the U.S.

I had met with the director and his sales agent in Duesseldorf where we worked out the details of our licensing agreement, first in his office and then later that evening at dinner. Later still we went to the old town to celebrate.

Pretty soon thereafter, tons of wood fiber mats were coming from Germany to be pressed into door and quarter panels at our Canandaigua plant.

What was astonishing was that our end product made with this material, although coming all the way from Germany and still needing to be pressed to panels and decorated here, was still more cost-effective than conventional polypropylene panels produced in the U.S.

And, as a bonus, we were also using renewable resources!

A few years later, some time after the wall had come down in Germany, I received a call from Lignotock inviting Don and me to come and visit their newest wood-fiber plant, which had just opened in the former East Germany section.

Don and I flew to Frankfurt where Eberhart picked us up and we drove to the new plant in the middle of the Thuringia forest to watch wood fiber mats being produced.

After the visit, we all decided to visit the new GM plant in Eisenach, a location where a few years earlier the old regime had built the East German Wartburg and Trabant model cars.

On the way to Eisenach, we drove past a huge barren mountain. Eberhart explained that waste products left over from the old Communist regime's uranium mines had been dumped there, and simply left.

Eberhart had managed to get us a king's tour of the newly built GM plant in the morning, and after lunch at their executive dining room we got an escort to take us to the old Wartburg castle up on the hill.

I had visited the castle when our two children were younger and knew of the steep path to get to it.

After about an hour walking up the hill Don looked flushed and said, "You guys go ahead. I'll wait here for you." He could go no further.

I knew then and there that something was wrong with Don's heart, and after our return to Detroit I made sure he visited a heart specialist.

(Don did see a specialist, who told him he had an irregular heartbeat and needed to take it easy if he wanted to reach retirement age. Unfortunately, Don could not change his lifestyle, and a few years later we lost him to a heart attack. That was a sad day for me.)

As a prudent policy, we started to look at Weyerhaeuser to develop wood fiber sources here in the U.S. as soon as we started with the production phase of the Beretta panels.

The whole Beretta program was a real success story for Voplex. The Lapeer, Michigan, plant molded the A posts in color and produced the instrument clusters with the glove box and knee bolster panels.

The Canandaigua plant produced the door and quarter panels and the package shelf. JP Emco molded the big rear bench seat with two storage compartments, and then carpet-covered it at their plant in Oklahoma – and all of it came together nicely at the assembly plant in Flint Michigan.

With a flash of marketing savvy, I had our design origin department mock-up a model of the Beretta interior for show and tell. It was a beauty and it cost, if I remember correctly, $17,500 to build.

And it was worth every penny because of all the positive publicity we got.

I also used Dick's Photography Studio located on Stevenson Highway to make high-gloss photos of all our products for show and tell.

Ron, our "handy man" helper, was in charge of the model, and he set it up with pictures and capability statements to showcase our engineering and manufacturing expertise at technical shows.

Voplex never received even one complaint about the quality of the Beretta plastic parts we supplied!

I believe that this program represented only the second time that the complete interior of a new model was sourced to one supplier. (The first was the Chrysler Minivan interior, awarded to DPM).

Unfortunately, again, the promised volumes did not materialize because the small Japanese cars, now coming to the U.S. in large volumes, were taking our business away. ("They are eating our lunch!" was what we said at the time.)

In Europe I had read a confidential study commissioned by an auto maker in the late 1980s that estimated the Japanese car industry (with their "in-house" supplier base) had a cost advantage over U.S. car makers of between $2,000 and $2,500 – and in Europe it was between $500 and $700 – per car.

This price difference was hard to overcome no matter how hard they squeezed us suppliers and how much in rebates the Big Three offered.

And in addition, in many cases the quality of the cars the Japanese produced and brought over was better than the vehicles we produced here in North America!

Part of my duty at Voplex and VHC was to put a rolling five- year plan and forecast together.

This was a new task to me since it was something that we never had done at DPM.

Mike's philosophy had been different. "You guys bring in the business and I will think about it and find the place and the machines to make the parts! (And should there be a recession coming up in the next year or two then we'll just send the people home.)"

I went through a very fast, but in-depth, learning phase.

I subscribed to Wards and other car production forecasters, such as DRI, and with Don's help, got a comprehensive study together, which Don presented to the board of directors at Voplex and later to the VHC board.

I stood by and made mental notes on how to do this on my own in the future. On subsequent annual meetings I was able to do the forecasts by myself as well as present the findings to the Board members. I still have a box full of those presentation foils and slides in my basement.

Don was also a great showman who believed in putting on big presentations about our capabilities for our customers.

Whenever I was in town he arranged presentations that got me in front of engineers, stylists, or purchasing people to talk about what we were doing, and the new technologies from Europe we were bringing back to save them money and weight.

Don encouraged my travel to Europe and told me to continue my friendships with other German and European companies.

At a meeting of the German plastics engineers in Baden-Baden, I met the manager of Menzolit Fibron, the plastics division of Dynamit Nobel. (Happich also owned part of Menzolit through a 60% ownership in Fibron).

We got along well and he invited me to his plant in Bretten, which I gladly accepted. He was very proud and showed me their progress with long fiber and polypropylene-molding technology, which I found far advanced compared to our studies and developments here in the U.S.

I stood by the machine, talked to the operator and took lots of notes and pictures, because I felt this technology was something that would give us a new advantage over our U.S. competition.

(I felt like one of those Japanese engineers I had escorted through our plants years before.) It would allow us to strengthen car bumpers significantly and reduce weight at the same time.

He invited me to stay at his house, where I met his wife and spent an enjoyable weekend.

I had been scheduled to give a presentation at that meeting about "in-mold foil molding," something that VW and other European OEMs were interested in for their exterior fascias and spoiler programs.

During my presentation my cell phone started to ring. Cell phones were, at that time, pretty rare in Europe. It was Ursula, wanting to know how and what I was doing. No matter how hard I tried to tell her to hang up, Ursula kept talking. I was embarrassed, but the audience did not seem to mind and many people came up to me after my talk, curious about the phone. As a result, I made many more contacts, which helped me with our European developments.

The VW engineers were impressed by how far advanced we were already with the "in-mold" technology and invited me to come to Wolfsburg, Germany where they would set up a meeting with a larger group of engineers and designers.

We introduced the long fiber technology here in the U.S. one year later.

We used it on our bumper system successfully, and shortly thereafter we started our joint venture with Menzolit Fibron.

This venture opened the Asian market for us as Menzolit had ventures with Hanwha and Ushihama Kassei in Korea. And in the following year we had Korean and German engineers going with us to visit our customers, showing our global strength.

In return, I flew a number of times to Seoul to go with Hanwha engineers to Hyundai and Kia to impress their peers with talk about our international capabilities.

What I did not like was the long flight to Korea, at the time only available via Tokyo from Detroit with a long layover at the Tokyo Airport. The seven- or eight-hour flight to and from Europe was long enough for me.

There was something interesting I noticed while I was in Korea. All new Korean cars being driven on the streets in Seoul were differently styled and appeared brand new to me.

I asked my friends from Hanwha and they told me that these models would be introduced to the Western world a couple of years later. They were obviously street-testing these new vehicles for at least a year prior to sending them over to the U.S.

A very smart move, I thought! Something else I learned dealing with Korean business people: they use the word "Ya-Ya" often. I found out that Ya-Ya means, "I hear you." It also means "I understand you," and it can additionally mean, "I agree with you!" No wonder in the early days there were a lot of confused European or American business people in those meetings!

During this period our engineers and the engineers of the various car companies were all busy looking for more ways to convert traditional used materials to less costly and lighter plastic materials, as increasing the content weight of plastic meant reducing the weight of the car to improve fuel efficiency.

CHAPTER 13: The Voplex Decline

Our daughter Karin, after completing high school at Anchor Bay in New Baltimore, had decided to attend Michigan Central University in Mount Pleasant to study psychology.

The school was about a four-hour drive away, but close enough for her to come home on weekends to have Mom do her laundry. Smart girl!

During the weekends she stayed home with us, I had many discussions and arguments with her regarding my capitalistic ways. Some of her professors tried to convince her that communism was the only acceptable way for the future to have an organized and civil world order.

I, on the other hand, having had first-hand exposure to the evil and dictatorial ways of communism, managed, after many heated discussions to set her straight.

During the summer months Karin worked at Salt River Golf Course on 23 Mile Road, where she met John Amatangelo. John was the son of one of the two brothers who owned the golf course and a bowling alley in New Baltimore. The two of them fell in love and they got married on December 2, 1989, after Karen had graduated.

As she had done with Andrew's wedding, Ursula put herself in charge to make all the arrangements!

However, this time it was different. Our circle of family and friends was relatively small. No matter how hard we tried we could not come up with a list of more than sixty people to invite.

It was a different story for John's mother on the Amatangelo side. Rose kept saying that it was difficult, if not impossible, for her to keep the number of invitations to fewer than 200.

Jokingly, I told Ursula to go out on 23 Mile Road, flag down cars, and hand out invitations to make the count more even.

In the end, however, nobody cared about the numbers of wedding guests and everyone we cared about were invited.

The ceremonies were performed in the same two churches that performed Lois and Andrew's wedding. The reception was held at the Monte Carlo Hall on Van Dyke and 23 Mile Road – in the middle of a snowstorm!

Karin and John left on their honeymoon to the Cayman Islands – where, unfortunately, Karin caught a rare viral infection and bacterial pneumonia. They had to fly back early because of her high fever, and we almost lost her because they could not figure out what strain of pneumonia had attacked her and how to cure it. She was in the hospital for almost a month before modern antibiotics finally took hold.

As I write this, a little more than 27 years later, Karin is still happily married to John, with three children in college. But she never worked a day at what she studied 4 years in college for.

Go figure!

In 1988 Mr. Landers, bowing under pressure from one of the major stockholders who was looking for a greater return on his investment, hired a chief executive officer to replace him.

After a hastily conducted executive search, the choice was a man named Joe who had been an executive at Rockwell.

Joe knew everything about torsion bars and steel springs. The plant he had been in charge of had specialized in producing these parts for heavy trucks.

Unfortunately, he had no knowledge about plastics, trim and colors, or new composite materials. Nor was he interested in learning. But we quickly learned that he liked to travel and play golf.

He brought new control systems into our plants that did not work for us because they were more geared to what he knew – which was metal-processing systems, which were not suitable for our multi-colored and diverse plastic materials processing plants.

But, what was worse, he begun spending money that the company did not have on things that we simply did not need; while at the same time refusing to invest in new machinery and technology that we *did* need to stay competitive.

Slowly, but surely, during the next two years Voplex drifted towards bankruptcy.

Our suppliers quickly picked up that we were stretching our accounts payable terms, and rumors began to circulate that things were not well with Voplex. They scrambled to cover themselves.

Around the middle of October, 1991, BFG, the approved vinyl supplier for our body side moldings, put VHC on a COD (cash on delivery) basis, and threatened to stop vinyl shipments altogether unless Chrysler's purchasing agent signed a letter guaranteeing payment.

That went over like a lead balloon!

Chrysler requested that Otto Happich, Joe, myself, and the Manager from BFG sit down to straighten things out. Otto flew in and he ended up agreeing that the Happich Corporation would guarantee payments to BFG.

I have to say here, and I have said this every time anyone wants to hear it, Otto Happich is one of the finest gentlemen I have ever known. I can't count the number of times he helped VHC with a phone call or a personal visit to get us out of a jam.

He has amassed a great circle of influential automotive friends worldwide. And he has helped me personally as well. Over the years Otto and his wife Brigitte became friends with Ursula and me and to this day we visit each other when they are here in the U.S., or we are in Wuppertal.

As a sideline, threatening Chrysler did the manager at BFG no good either. BFG fired him about a month later.

Ursula called me at my office on October 20th. Thank God I was in town. She told me that she had stomach pains. I called an ambulance to go to the house and met them at the hospital. Her appendix was inflamed and needed to be taken out right away!

She was operated on that afternoon and recovered nicely in a few days. That was a scary day for me!

On a more joyful note, on the 31st of October Katherine Louise Amatangelo, our first grandchild, was born.

I remember vividly telling Ursula and Karin that at only 55 years old, I was too young to be a grandfather!

But nobody paid any attention to me or cared about what I thought.

All things considered, the uncertain future of Voplex made it very difficult to get new work from our customers and, on the 17th of August 1992, Voplex declared bankruptcy and filed for reorganization.

Here I was again, now 56 years old, facing an uncertain future!

During the six years that I worked for Don, I had invested a considerable amount of my own money into Voplex stock, which overnight became worthless.

Well, I told Ursula and myself, buying Voplex stock had seemed like a good idea at the time. My tax accountant told me to look at the bright side. "You will probably never run out of using these losses on the loss-forward portions of your annual tax returns."

⌘⌘⌘

But Voplex was saved from the scrap heap. Our savior, Richard Crawford, walked into our offices sometime in April 1993, accompanied by two partners. He had managed against considerable odds and quite a number of other bidders to satisfy the bankruptcy court.

He now owned Voplex, lock, stock and barrel.

And he also took over the 50% Voplex portion of the VHC joint venture.

I am an engineer, and I know a lot of stuff, but these financial dealings were way above me. Still, I freely admit here, I would like to have had the knowledge to pull off something like that for my own benefit.

Richard, who I admire, has a solidly good character. He is loyal and very smart. He is self-made, hardworking, always thinking, and truly an entrepreneur.

He started the Purple Pickle restaurant chain on 8 Mile Road, West of Gratiot in Detroit when he was in high school, and after graduating from college became a homebuilder and developer. He developed home sites north of 23 Mile Road in the Schoenherr area. Around 1985 he decided to enter the automotive supply business as a supplier. He is 10 years younger than I am.

I thought after meeting him that my European and U.S. plastics and automotive knowledge and his financial strength and entrepreneurial know-how would make us a good team, and that we could return Voplex to its former glory. Indeed, Richard kept me; but he decided to let Don go.

That was a sad day for me. Don had been a mentor and a true friend to me.

Don understood Richard's decision, and a short time later he went to work for one of our competitors.

At one of my early meetings with Richard he told me that he had read about new plastic gas tanks and asked if that was something we should be pursuing.

I advised against it because I knew the lead engineer at the Ford Saline/Milan plastic plant, and I knew the struggles they were having with blow-molding plastic tanks. There were still a lot of problems with selecting the proper plastic material combinations for the tanks.

It took another five years before engineers perfected a seven-layer plastic material that convinced the safety engineers that a plastic gas tank was a safe and viable replacement for a metal tank. And then another considerable weight and cost savings was achieved!

(Shortly after Richard took over Voplex, we moved from Troy and consolidated our offices in Dearborn where Richard had purchased Universal Plastics in1986, Nortec in 1988, and Wolf Engineering in 1990.

All three companies were producing small, functional under-the-hood parts for the auto industry with sales of about $20 million.

Small functional parts would become another gold mine for supplanting metal with plastic parts. There are thousands of small plastic functional parts situated throughout the modern automobile.

The engine and transmission of every U.S. car rolling off an assembly line today uses a variety of highly-specialized plastic materials on small parts to ensure their viability and longevity.

Richard told me at our very first meeting that we would conduct business as usual. And this became our new battle cry: Voplex and VHC are alive, financially viable, and are producing good parts!

And we also now had three respected high-precision injection molders in our fold!

We all got along well and Richard soon asked me to be the sales manager as well as taking care of VHC in Woodstock.

VHC was also doing well, Chrysler was happy, and we were getting requests to quote body side moldings from other companies.

Two programs were of interest to us.

Volkswagen in Puebla, Mexico had designed a new Golf/ Jetta body side molding, and Hyundai needed body side moldings for their Sonata model to be produced in their factory in Sherbrook, Quebec, north of Montreal. After many visits we were successful in getting both programs and Happich started making the required tools.

I flew to Germany with the Hyundai quality engineers as we tried out the tools, made samples in Wuppertal, got them approved, and then transferred the tools to Woodstock.

I brought some of the new small tools and checking fixtures with me to Canada in a specially made hard leather case (that case is also still in my basement today).

Both jobs started out well; Hyundai was an easy customer. They liked what they saw right from the start and continued taking our moldings for two years (produced in seven different colors, with no stabilizer and double-sided gummed tape on four different parts).

Then someone at their South Korea head office decided to mothball the entire plant in Sherbrook.

Nobody ever figured out why they did that, and all the supervisors and managers, who loved living near Montreal, hated having to go back to South Korea.

And we hated to lose this good-paying, easy work.

Working for VW in Mexico was by no means as easy! It required many trips for me to Puebla as well as to Wolfsburg.

The laboratory in Wolfsburg wanted to be closely involved in the testing of the vinyl moldings. They were interested in the fact that our parts were being exposed to the elements in the Navaho Desert.

Their lab specialist had our body side moldings exposed at an angle of exactly 45 degrees facing east at sunrise and then following the sun by a computerized steering system all day long.

They were exposed in this way for 45 days. What they were testing for was to assure themselves that the colors on the moldings would not fade or change.

Only Germans would test moldings that way.

But our parts passed all the tests and we started shipping them to Mexico in cardboard containers on wooden pallets.

(A couple of years later we proposed sending the parts in returnable containers as a cost saving. This almost created a riot and was overwhelmingly rejected – this is because, we found out, the workers at the VW plant in Puebla took our empty packaging and used it in home construction for their families. These newly-built cardboard huts could readily be seen then, perched on the hills (without any running tap water, electricity, or sanitary sewers) outside of Mexico City on the highway to Puebla.)

CHAPTER 14: The Ascent of Cambridge

I was still traveling to Germany and the rest of Europe at regular intervals to stay in touch with Happich as well as my contacts at the German auto companies and their plastic parts suppliers. Plastics technology was advancing rapidly in Europe and we wanted to be part of that and, where possible, to transfer this technology to the U.S.

Sometime in the fall of 1993, I had met Peter Strohmeier at a plastic seminar in Paris. Peter was the CEO of EMPE, located in Geretsried near Bad Toelz, south of Munich in Bavaria. EMPE, at that time, was still a privately owned supplier of interior plastic trim parts.

Their three main customers were BMW, Mercedes, and Opel.

They had specialized in door and quarter panels, package shelves and headliners – some injection-molded, but mostly compression-molded and covered with leather or cloth. Their sales were around DM 100.00 million (about $50 million)

What was of special interest was that they used a polypropylene and flax fiber-mat, compression-molded (which did not require polyester as a binding agent), as the structural portion of the panels, shelves, and headliner assemblies.

Peter and I met a number of times and, sometime late in 1993, I convinced Richard that a joint venture between Cambridge, (which Richard had named our new company after Wolf, Nortec Universal, and Voplex had come together) and EMPE would benefit both companies in Europe as well as in the U.S., Canada, and Mexico.

After looking over the contract that our lawyers had prepared, Richard and I flew to Frankfurt and then on to Munich, rented a car and drove to Geretsried. We signed the contract that afternoon in Peter's office.

And so, the new joint venture company, CEATS was born.

By the way, I lay claim to the name. On the way over on the plane, I thought about a catchy name and I put this together:

C would stand for Cambridge, E would be for EMPE, A for Automotive, T for Trim, and S for Systems. It took me a while to convince Richard and Peter; but in the end they agreed.

We celebrated the signing of the venture at the Alte Post Hotel in Bad Toelz that evening with a really good Bavarian meal and a tasty bottle of wine.

Richard did not drink alcohol and Peter Strohmeier had only one glass to be social, so I ended up drinking the rest. But I was happy and slept well that night.

At breakfast the next morning, we decided that one of the EMPE engineers should right away be transferred to Cambridge.

Sometime in March of 1993, I had learned that a plant in Trenton was planning to exit their $300m plastic extrusion business and I mentioned this at one of our VHC board meetings.

Richard told me to go there and talk to the people. Otto and I flew to Trenton on March 12th and visited the huge, sprawling old factory. The monstrous 1.1 million sq. foot facility sat on 82 acres, and had 1850 unionized employees.

There were five business units associated with the plant. Extrusion with 11 lines, injection molding with 23 molding machines, the handles and seat adjuster assembly, the glass business, and the powder coating.

At the time the plant's equipment was less than 50% utilized. They had an official 6% to 8% of the workforce absent every day; and their payroll function was outsourced.

The plant was losing money, and Mr. Lopez, the head of Global Purchasing at GM, was telling them that they had to lower their prices!

We realized very quickly that they were trying to unload the plant at almost any price.

Otto and I took about three hours with them, to be polite, then turned around and took the next flight back to Detroit. It proved to me again that not everything offered for sale is necessarily a good thing. As the saying goes, "Not all that glitters is gold. I found out later that nobody bought that old plant and it shut down less than 2 years later.

Sometime in January of 1994 I had a chance to meet Mr. Lopez, just before he left GM and went to work for VW.

I had been invited to the opening of the new Johnson Control plant, which made seats for GM in Portugal.

I knew the CEO of Jonson Control (we supplied functional parts for their seats), and he and I thought, with our connection, it would be a good idea to be there.

The new plant had been built in Nelas, Portugal, and on the 19th January I listened to Lopez give his standard pep talk about lean engineering, getting leaner every month, giving back every year, and being grateful to be included in his supply chain.

I had never liked him because of what I perceived as his manipulative supplier relationship philosophy, and that speech confirmed my dislike. He was every supplier's nightmare!

His canned speech was given in English and Spanish. His handlers apparently had forgotten to tell him that the people in Portugal speak Portuguese, not Spanish.

I truly believe that Mr. Lopez did more damage to the relationship between the automotive companies and their supply base than any other purchasing executive.

The only benefit of the trip was that I got to enjoy the beautiful Portuguese countryside in the spring, driving to Nelas and back to Lisbon where I stayed the night.

⌘⌘⌘

While I was away Richard had not been sitting idle.

He had found us a new two-story office building, with plenty of room for Cambridge management, engineering, design, CATIA engineers and sales staff on 13-½ Mile Road, just east of I-75 (a stone's throw away from our old Voplex offices, north of 14 Mile Road).

Additionally, he had been in negotiations for the better part of a year with Rockwell and had made them an offer to take their composite plastic division off their hands. They had finally agreed to sell.

All of that happened in March of 1994 and we increased our sales from $100 to $300 million practically overnight.

That would have been OK if the basic technology had been the same for us thermo-plastic people. However, that was no longer the case.

Suddenly, the majority of our sales were derived from thermoset plastic, consisting of SMC, BMC, GMT and GRU. These were all materials that we, the "old Cambridge" people, were unfamiliar with.

The Rockwell plants, which we now owned, were located in Centralia, Illinois; Lenoir, North Carolina; and Shelbyville, Indiana.

But also interesting — and scary — was that our customer base was so different – and included the heavy truck business.

Rockwell had been molding large parts for Freightliner, Mack, Volvo, Kenwood, as well as Ford and GM Trucks.

Because of the complexity of the products and diversity of the processes and customers, Richard quickly decided to form four divisions, with Kevin Alder (who had come with the Rockwell acquisition) as president.

- Tom, who came from the Centralia plant, was to run the exterior products division;
- Pat, who had been the plant manager at the Lapeer plant was to run our (old) interior trim systems;
- Pat, who had been the plant manager at the Lapeer plant, would run the commercial truck division, and
- my old friend Terry would run the industrial products division.

I had known Terry from 1984 to 1988 when he was the plant manager at DPM's 15-Mile plant. He was a very talented production manager and had previously been a GM engineer, later working with DeLorean to build the plant in Ireland where they produced the DeLorean Gullwing sports car!

And I was to continue developing new leads for mergers, acquisitions and joint ventures, managing VHC, and reporting directly to Richard. For the first time in many years I was no longer connected to direct sales!

There were a couple of really interesting and revolutionary plastic developments that came to us from the Rockwell acquisition.

The first one was the all-plastic cross-car beam, which was supporting the instrument panel. It replaced 20 individual steel parts, incorporated all air ducts, and stabilized the instrument panel while reducing the weight of the combined parts by 40%.

It produced a 35% savings over the previous parts' cost!

The other new development was a rocker arm cover-molded with a short fiberglass-filled resin, with a second-stage, molded-on seal. This part also eliminated 20 different metal parts and reduced weight by 2 lbs. (48%). This, too, of course was a huge cost saving.

At the time of our Rockwell purchase, the Centralia plant had just finished the work on a complete SMC (sheet molding compound) truck bed for Ford. This project was also a total success. It reduced both the weight and the cost of the truck bed by more than 40% over the metal version. This truck bed, because it was plastic, was also very quiet – and customers just loved it!

Another astonishing Ford product at the Centralia plant was the production of a complete one-piece SMC roof molding for one of their SUV models that included both the A and the C posts.

Through the Rockwell purchase, Cambridge now had 26% of the SMC North American automotive market. Our closest competitor at this time was Budd with a16% market share.

But Richard had set his sights even higher.

He purchased the thermoset business of Gen Corp later in 1996; and Eagle Pitcher and Goodyear's plastic business became Cambridge business by 1997.

That gave Cambridge 43% of the exterior plastic market and our sales were approaching $500 million. We served nearly every automobile and truck maker in the USA, Canada, and Mexico.

And by that time the average plastic content on a North American built vehicle was close to 500 pounds!

Just think, in the span of roughly 30 years the plastic content of the automobile had grown from 25 pounds to almost 500 pounds! An increase of 2000%!

But what that number does not reveal is the astonishing reduction in the weight of the automobile – and the accompanying increase in fuel efficiency as well as the numerous additions of occupant safety-related parts – as plastic replaced the heavier metal materials.

What a coincidence in numbers: Cambridge was selling $500 million in plastic parts to the car industry and there were now close to 500 pounds of plastic on a vehicle!

And our plastic parts supply business still had a lot of room to grow!

You may have noticed that my terminology in this narrative has switched from "cars" to "vehicles" for the first time. This is because trucks at this time became huge users of glass-reinforced thermoset plastic materials.

By 1997, the hoods, fenders, doors, side panels, spoilers, and roofs on large trucks — and in some cases on buses — were being designed with plastic materials in mind. These parts use an incredible amount of plastic material and the low cost of the tooling, as compared to traditional metal tools and parts, allowed any truck manufacturer to change the look of a model quite frequently; and, at the same time, very cost effectively.

During this time the car companies also made use of the glass-filled "load bearing" capability of thermoset materials.

Again due to the relatively low tooling costs and part price reductions involved in the compression-molding process, we were awarded the production order for the load floor of a GM sporty muscle cars, which would be made with a special directional glass-reinforced polyester.

A little later we also received the order for the load floor for a new Chrysler sports car. We also produced the hoods, doors, and fenders for these sports car models with thermoset plastic materials.

We produced these parts in one of our smaller shops, again inherited from Rockwell; it was located on Mound Road in Warren, Michigan.

I remember the many challenges we had with both of the hoods, because of the high visibility and the sheer size of the part. The glass in polyester has a nasty habit of wanting to "float" to the surface, and by doing so, leaves little holes in it that cannot be covered with paint. And every time that happens the part ends up being scrapped.

Thank goodness the yearly volume of these sport car models was low.

But, I am getting ahead of myself regarding another European development – and another huge innovation for the plastics industry.

⌘⌘⌘⌘

To go back a couple of years, in June of 1994 I had traveled to Menningen in Southern Germany to meet with Klaus of Flexiflies, who had previously constructed the Flax/PP machine for the EMPE plant in Geretsried.

I reviewed the improved process and asked Dick from our Canandaigua plant to fly over and confirm my review. He liked what he saw. We negotiated a price and bought the machine, had it crated up, and sent it to the Canandaigua plant.

To explain, the machine mashes and then separates the straw from the linen (flax) fibers on the one side of the machine, then discards the straw and feeds in the spun polypropylene fibers onto the other side, bringing the two materials together at the desired ratio. It then needles a woven mat about six feet wide, which is at the end of the machine rolled up. It allowed us to regulate the percentage of the individual materials to the product or customers' requirement.

We went through the U.S. approval process and – lo and behold – at the start of the 1995 model car production, we were making and shipping door- and quarter-panels with a flax/polypropylene mixture.

We replaced the woodchip/polyester Lignotock material – at a further cost and weight savings to our GM customer.

We purchased the flax straw from the Cargill Co. in Manitoba, Canada.

I had visited Cargill in August that year and negotiated a relatively low price for the straw, which until then was burned in the fields after the linseed pods were harvested.

This type of straw with fibers is a waste product because the fibers are too short to be used for linen, and the straw, which will not rot away in the fields, needs to be burned after the harvest. The result was that miles and miles of burning and smoke-filled fields polluted the air and darkened the area.

And here was another lesson I learned! A product is only a waste product as long as nobody has a use for it!

The price I negotiated included delivery of the straw from Manitoba to our plant in Canandaigua. So shortly after that, we had a lot of railcars bringing flax fiber straw from Canada to our plant in New York State.

Since nobody in the U.S. had a like product, Richard asked me to file a patent for Empeflex (this is what I called the polypropylene-flax fiber mixture) under the Cambridge name.

Understandably, the price for the flax fibers went up the following year as the straw no longer was a waste product: the demand for it increased because all the car companies wanted to have these cheaper lightweight panels. And competitors like Magna and Lear Corp. soon purchased machines like ours from Germany and brought them to the U.S.

The product was here to stay and is still in use today!

Other renewable fibers from banana or hemp have also been tried and used, but none have proven better than the incredibly strong linen fiber.

CHAPTER 15: Chickening Out on Further Growth

To jump back a bit, at the end of June of 1994 at a VHC board meeting at Happich in Wuppertal, Otto told me that Happich had decided to exit their exterior business, and asked if Cambridge was interested in buying it.

This news came as a real shock to me.

I learned from Otto that the driving force behind this move was his cousin, the silent side of the business, who owned the other half of the Happich Company.

This cousin had kept in the background all this time, letting Otto run the company, but had decided that this was a good time to sell, as he thought Happich would soon begin to lose money at their location in Wuppertal.

I still believe, and Otto agreed with me, that he just wanted to get out and get as much money out of the company as possible.

Otto's idea was that Happich would sell the exterior business to Cambridge; then they would concentrate on their interior business in a joint venture with an American company making sun visors, mirrors, and handles.

I told Otto that I could not speak for Richard but that this, in my mind, made sense and would be a golden opportunity for Cambridge by having a foothold in the exterior business in Europe.

Cambridge could then go after the truck business from Mercedes, MAN, Renault, and all the other European truck manufacturers with facilities in Germany. I spoke excitedly about this opportunity when I returned and met with Richard the following week. Richard was also very enthusiastic.

Unfortunately, it did not happen! Richard had set up a meeting the day after I returned to Detroit with Kevin and his executive staff to discuss the opportunity for us to have a European location.

But Kevin felt that an internal shortage of knowledgeable managers and technicians would not allow him and his staff to manage or support a manufacturing site in Europe at that time.

He told us flat out that he had trouble running the corporation as it was now, and any involvement in Europe would (as he put it) "bring this house of cards down."

We argued for most of the day, and in the end Richard and I lost the argument. I knew then that Kevin was shortsighted and unable to leave his comfort zone. (Part of his argument was that none of his managers – all southern U.S. boys – had any interest in, or wanted to work at, a facility in Europe).

Looking back now, I am convinced that this was the single biggest strategic mistake Richard made while owning Cambridge. I firmly believe that with the right manager and a competent staff in place running our manufacturing sites, we could have beaten Magna to the punch and become the world's largest plastics supplier to the auto industry.

We had the opportunity and we missed it. We were that close!

Consider, too, that earlier that year Richard and I had met with the president and vice president of Sommer Allibert in Paris to discuss a joint venture. They were at the time the largest producer of instrument panels in Europe.

I had met the two of them at the Paris Plastic Conference that April, and we'd talked about the opportunities that working together could offer both companies.

We discussed in detail the set-up of two separate companies. One would create an interior trim system branch and the other an exterior business venture. Both companies were to be run by the partners in their respective countries, reporting to the board. Shares of the new joint venture would be issued based on the true value of each individual company.

Sommer Allibert was very interested in such an arrangement because it provided them an entry to the North American market and Cambridge wanted an entry to the European market. It looked like a feasible partnership at the time!

Cambridge had become an important "Tier One" company in North America. We had all the plastic technical know-how to be a valued and respected supplier. GM had selected us "Supplier of the Year" for the previous three years. And Richard had just been named "entrepreneur of the year" by the State of Michigan!

Cambridge was now supplying parts to almost all of the North American automotive OEM companies. We supplied parts to the original "Big Three" companies for all of their models, all six of the transplant companies, and nine heavy-truck manufacturers.

We were producing every conceivable interior plastic part, whether injection-molded, compression-molded, blow-molded, slush-molded or extrusion-molded. We were molding functional parts like bumper beams, radiator frames, valve covers, cross-vehicle beams, oil pans, fans, pump housings – and all sizes and types of gears and ball-bearing retainers with the newest and specialized materials.

In addition, at that time, we were the only company approved to produce a complete-load floor for two sports cars.

A load floor is a critical part of the automobile. As the name suggests, the integrity and safety of the entire passenger compartment rests on this part. As you can imagine, extreme care has to be taken as the material is prepared and the part is molded.

And after the molding process, every part had to be individually inspected and tested. We were molding these parts with a special-woven directional glass mat saturated with polyester.

I was at this plant one day watching the process with some of our engineering customers when I remembered an older Kaiser model car purchased by my cousin Manfred back in 1958 or '59 in Sarnia, Ontario.

On the passenger side, you could see the street through rusted-out holes in the floor. Manfred had simply put a wooden board there. But I knew that now, thanks to plastics, this would never happen again!

For the exterior of the North American cars and trucks, Cambridge was molding front ends, fenders, hoods, roofs, spoilers, air deflectors, cowls, side panels, rear and side doors, and body-side moldings.

There was not a plastic part on a car or truck that Cambridge did not or could not mold, finish and ship to a manufacturer!

⌘⌘⌘

The inspiration for this book was to reflect upon how the automobile went from being comprised of a few pounds of plastic in 1965 to incorporating over 500 pounds by the late 1990s!

I got to witness this dramatic development in the 30-plus years that I had the good fortune to be personally and intimately involved in both the industry's failures and its successes.

Back in 1995, just over 16 million vehicles were being produced in North America. The industry provided a very lucrative business for the handful of raw plastic material manufacturers.

In September of 1997 Richard asked Terry Werrell and me to fly to San Paolo, Brazil and drive about 60 miles west to Rio Claro to visit an Owens Corning molding plant there.

Owens Corning had a big glass fiber-producing plant there and at one time had built a small molding plant next door to it; I believe it was to test their glass fibers. Now the molding plant was for sale.

Terry looked the plant over and found it created an opportunity for Cambridge in Brazil. I contacted the Brazilian auto and truck manufactures and they all said they would give us work if we had a manufacturing facility in the country.

So we told Richard to buy it and a deal was made a few months later. Terry had promised Richard he could run the plant with his eyes closed. Richard bought it without telling his timid Operations Director, Kevin.

I convinced Vince, who had joined our company a year earlier, to move to San Paulo to be our sales engineer in Brazil.

Vince was a very likable young man and he did very well getting us new work from the various auto, truck and – very important – bus-producing companies in Brazil.

Being in Brazil was a very positive development. First, all the OEM's liked having their suppliers next door, and secondly our joint venture partners in Europe wanted to be able to claim they had factory space there.

So, pretty soon Arno from Menzolit, Ansgar from EMPE, and I from Cambridge were knocking on Brazilian OEM's doors, looking for new business.

And in Brazil it worked well for us because a lot of European OEM's who had never heard of Cambridge, but who knew EMPE and Menzolit Fibron, needed plastic component parts made in Brazil for their trucks.

CHAPTER 16: Going Modular - 500+ lbs.

The next hurdle for the "Tier One" supplier was to develop "modular" capabilities. This was around 1997. It meant being the supplier of a complete system.

For instance, the front-end module, when delivered just in time, consisted of the in-color produced fascia, the bumper beam with shock absorbers behind it, the grille with complete headlamp assembly (bulbs with wires, etc.), and the radiator frame with bezel housings and the fan frame.

These were now all-plastic parts welded, glued, or sometimes screwed together; albeit almost every part was made from a different plastic material.

The second stage of the development, which came about a year after the first, included the radiator, the fan, and all the hoses and electrical wires attached.

Another system being considered was what DuPont and DPM had tried to do about 12 years earlier: namely a complete door-panel assembly with a color-coded, painted outer door, including a door handle and lock, with a finished inner panel and the window-lift mechanism with the glass, the seals, the speakers, and all the electrical wiring attached.

Everything — except the glass, the outer metal door (in some cases), the seals, the speakers, and the wiring — was molded plastic!

A third system was our cross-car beam, being used to assemble the instrument panel, glove box, airbag, all ducts, wiring and the electronics together, and being shipped just-in-time to the assembly plant.

Then off course, all the seats in the car had become complete systems, only needing at the assembly plant to be attached to the floor pan and connected to the seat belt system and the various wire harnesses.

This had become the new normal for the auto companies and Tier One suppliers.

The automotive engineers gradually shifted more and more assembly work away from their traditional, higher cost OEM factories to the lower-cost supply base. The unions objected, but the onslaught of foreign cars to the North American market and the shrinking profit margins of the domestic OEMs made this technical and political development inevitable.

As the American workforce shrank, the UAW lost more and more members to early retirements and layoffs, weakening their bargaining position further. Power shifted away from American workers.

⌘⌘⌘

Like all big developments had before it, the move to modular systems required a very high financial commitment from participating suppliers. It required very capable design and engineering departments working hand in hand with the automakers' engineers.

It further required large facilities, and teams of people logistically able to bring all the components to the plants with the least amount of held inventory, and to assemble all the parts together, and finally ship the finished color-coded systems on a just-in-time basis.

What a difference this was to the "shot and ship in a box" days of the 60s, 70s, 80s – and even the early 90s.

There was eventually talk by car-company executives of using only a limited number of suppliers who would cluster close by their assembly plants, being electronically connected and able to manufacture, assemble, and supply these modules as they were required.

We had finally arrived at a point at which all the car companies would have to do was sell the finished cars.

Richard liked the idea of being a modular supplier and wanted Cambridge to be part of this development – but he also knew that Cambridge did not have sufficient capital to participate.

He asked me to put an investor presentation together, which I did; and in June of 1997 he and I flew to Boston on his private plane to meet with a well-known venture capital firm.

They were fascinating people and seemed genuinely interested in our proposal that they partner with Cambridge.

They told us they believed that the U.S. automotive supply base had a lot of growth potential, and considering that all developing engineering by the car companies was done in Detroit, they thought Cambridge had a very good chance of being such a special modular supplier.

However, in follow-up meetings they put a number of terms into the contract — regarding control of the company — which Richard could not agree to.

Or maybe, foreseeing what would happen a few years later, someone there was smart enough to stay away from the automotive industry!

By the middle of 1997, there was a development at the office in Detroit that changed everything for me. I started to have problems with Kevin.

Cambridge had grown very rapidly and our human resources were stretched to the limit. (And, in my not-so-humble opinion, Kevin did not hire talented people.)

My job, and I took it seriously, was to bring in potential new joint ventures or possible acquisitions.

At the same time, Kevin was having a hard time keeping Cambridge together at almost $600m in sales.

He was familiar with the people who worked with and under him, but he absolutely shied away from hiring any talented people that he did not know. My assessment was that he did not want anybody on his staff that could potentially endanger his position! With this attitude, it seemed to me at the time, he actively worked against Cambridge's further growth.

⌘⌘⌘

In the meantime at Happich, Hans Wolf had retired and the board had hired a financial advisor to replace him.

It did not take this man long to realize that the profit to be made was only if the entire Happich company were to be sold.

Happich, during the previous couple of years, had not grown along with the other plastic suppliers in Europe because the board had refused to grant Otto the money needed for new technology. Sales had been stagnant, the plant in Wuppertal was losing money, and the silent shareholders (family members) were unhappy.

The new advisor prepared an offering for a possible sale, and after a few months he received a positive answer from the Becker Group!

To this day, I don't know if the advisor organized it this way, but we had a VHC board meeting scheduled at their head office in Wuppertal on the same day that Chuck was meeting there to talk about the Happich sale.

It was almost comical. I was going down the hallway with Otto when a door opened and there was the Happich advisor with Chuck.

Chuck did a double take when he saw me with Otto. He blurted out: "Is Cambridge going after Happich too? With Otto on your side, what chance do I have?"

I told Chuck not to worry, and went on to my VHC board meeting with Otto. Afterwards we had an enjoyable luncheon.

But I bet my bottom dollar that Chuck paid a little more for Happich after our "chance" meeting in the hallway.

The whole affair started me thinking!

Here was the Becker Group, grown out of a plastic mold-making shop that we used at DPM many times when our own Paragon Tools company could not do a job for us, demonstrating the financial capability to purchase Happich after having purchased DPM out of bankruptcy some years earlier. I knew then that they had something we did not have. I knew that you could make money as a supplier to the auto companies if you had a very smart team running your company efficiently.

Anyway, the deal went through, and Chuck became the owner of Happich.

And with it, he had an established beachhead in Europe.

VHC became a wholly owned Cambridge facility, for which I was still 100% responsible!

We continued to produce moldings for Chrysler and VW, filling our twin-screw extruder capacity every year.

CHAPTER 17: Servicing the World

I was continuing to travel to Brazil and Europe to promote our company with our joint venture partners, and demonstrate our worldwide capabilities to the car companies. During this time I traveled on an almost weekly basis.

Volkswagen in Wolfsburg was developing the new "Beetle," with an "all plastic" body.

Unfortunately, their engineers had no knowledge about the different exterior plastic materials.

They had talked to plastic suppliers like Bayer, BASF, GE, and DuPont, all of whom had their own interests at the forefront (i.e. they wanted to sell their type of plastic) – and after listening to each of them the VW engineers were thoroughly confused.

I remember being at engineering meetings where the discussion involved using a soft plastic for the fenders and designing a much harder plastic hood right next to it.

I explained to them why this would not work. I showed them data to prove my point, and showed them what we did to solve the problem on truck bodies. I argued for two days until they finally understood.

It was a painful experience and I should have remembered beforehand how stubborn German engineers are. Many times, as I sat there listening I thought of the saying "Don't confuse me with facts; my mind is made up."

But good came out of all of this.

When the time came a couple of years later for the introduction of the new Beetle, I was invited by a Wolfsburg VW executive to come to Puebla with Ursula to help celebrate the occasion.

We stayed at the Meson del Angel Hotel in Puebla during the festivities. This is a charming Mexican hacienda-style hotel, with beautiful handmade tiles on the floors and walls. There were also security guards with big guns everywhere, including at all the functions. I have to say that VW did put on a safe and exiting show! We stayed there a full week.

The VW staff showed us around the area and took us to see the pyramids around Puebla (where they told us that all the secrets are still hidden in the chambers below).

When I got back to my office in Detroit the following Monday, a call waited for me from Mercedes in Brazil. They were designing a new model for their truck for the Brazilian market and wanted to know if the exterior plastic parts design was feasible – and if Cambridge was interested in making these parts.

So barely 24 hours later I said goodbye to Ursula, and turned right around and took the evening flight with Varig Air from New York to San Paulo.

I loved flying with Varig because business class was always upgraded to first class and they carved the roast beef at your seat. They also served caviar with ice-cold Russian vodka all evening.

(It was rough getting out of the plane in San Paulo in the morning and getting back to reality! Nothing is worse than leaving the San Paulo Airport with a hangover and driving for the better part of an hour along the foulest-smelling river in the world to get to the city.)

But once there I met with two Mercedes truck engineers and we discussed all day the plastic parts they had designed for their new truck model.

As is customary, we went to dinner late that evening and, as the Brazilians like to eat and socialize, I went to bed around two o'clock in the morning.

The next morning at 7 o'clock I received a call from Arno of Menzolit, who had tracked me down to ask if I could help with a spoiler being designed by BMW for their U.S. production in Spartanburg. Cambridge was naturally very interested in such a program.

So, I flew from San Paolo to Frankfurt in the evening and on to Munich the next morning. Arno picked me up and we drove to BMW to meet with three exterior design engineers.

They showed us their concept for the new spoiler on the vehicle. It was designed for the X 3, an SUV, and was to be located at the rear, on top of the roof, with the rear upper stoplight and other electronics like the GPS incorporated.

We discussed various options. A glued-together two-shell system like the one we built for the Mustang came to my mind immediately.

I called Tom at our Centralia plant to get him involved and to pursue this opportunity at their level in Spartanburg.

We agreed it would be great to produce parts made by Cambridge in the U.S. for BMW.

I had a late dinner with the BMW engineers and Arno that evening.

During that dinner, one of the BMW engineers revealed that they were experimenting with molding parts with a carbon fiber epoxy material for under-the-hood application in their Landshut facility and, if I had time, he could take me there in the morning.

I was very interested, since we had discussed similar projects at Cambridge. Very early in the morning (5:00 a.m.), he picked me up and we drove to their in-house plastics molding and testing facility. After signing a secrecy agreement I was escorted into their molding room.

What a fantastic place! There was everything that a plastics engineer could wish for – all the latest machines with all the technologies imaginable, and everybody walked around in white coats. I did see for the first time what looked like good parts being molded with carbon fibers.

I congratulated them on their success, thanked the engineers for showing me their progress on carbon-fiber molding, and assured them that I would return the favor by showing them around any of the Cambridge plants next time they visited the U.S.

Later that day I received a call from VW asking me to come back to Wolfsburg to talk about a newly-developed in-mold paint film for bumpers, and possibly for plastic fenders, which was one of my favorite topics at the time because of the cost savings involved.

I flew to Hanover, rented a car, and returned to Wolfsburg, where I met with a number of senior exterior design engineers and explained the pros and cons associated with the process of applying a paint film into the injection-molding process.

I warned them that, because of contour and undercuts, not every part was suitable for this process. I even showed them some "cannot do" examples on some bumper fascia parts.

To further demonstrate the breakneck pace at which things were moving for us at this time, while at the meeting with the engineers in Wolfsburg I received a call from my secretary that an old friend from Ford Motor who was now purchasing parts for Ford of Europe wanted to talk to me.

When I called back he asked me since I was in Europe if I could "go by" and help with some problems they were having with a wood supplier to their Jaguar brand, who was located in England.

Knowing that we could help with our real wood joint venture plant located in Bergamo, Italy, I agreed to meet him the following morning in his office near London. I flew into Heathrow that evening and stayed at the Sheraton Airport hotel.

After all that travel I arrived around midnight, dead tired. I went straight to my room, and went to sleep.

At about 1:30 a.m. I woke up to go the bathroom. I got up, went through the door that I thought led to the bathroom, and heard a sickening click as it closed behind me.

I was startled wide awake as I realized that I was standing in the hallway in front of my closed hotel room door - in my underpants!

After what seemed like an eternity, I got the courage to take the elevator down to the lobby. Unfortunately, I had to pass by the lobby bar, which was still open at that time; and I got quite a lot of laughs and some raunchy comments from bar patrons as I walked by.

But this was not the end of the dilemma. When I got to the reception, I had no clue what my room number was. Luckily, however, I could still remember my name.

The night manager kindly gave me a robe and escorted me back to my room. After I'd finally gone to the bathroom, it took quite a while for me to get back to sleep.

This was only one of the many adventures I had tearing around Europe, often sleep-deprived, on behalf of Cambridge.

The next morning I took a taxi to the Ford offices, talked to my old friend, and got the ball rolling on fixing the wood issue on the Jaguar.

During the past year Jaguar had, in order to save a little money, changed from real wood to an "ink floating on water" over a plastic part process, which, when finished, simulated real wood. But the process had not worked out as planed and Jaguar was receiving complaints from some customers. Peter Strohmeyer promised to send an engineer with real wood samples and I left.

I called Diane at our office and asked her to get me home on the next available plane.

In a relatively short period I had traveled to Mexico, Brazil, Germany, England and, finally, I was waiting to go home. I had met with engineers and buyers from Mercedes, BMW, VW, and Ford; had late dinners every night; eaten and drunk too much; and gotten little sleep.

I was tired. I was over 60 years old and for the first time I could really feel my age. My body told me that it was getting near time to take it easy—but most of all it told me that it needed a rest. Servicing the whole world was a job for a younger man.

When I got home I made arrangements for Ursula and me to fly to Jamaica. I needed a beach.

We rented a place at the ocean and swam every day in the azure blue Caribbean Sea.

One day we decided to climb the famous Jamaican waterfalls with about 20 tourists, most of them much younger than I was. We got into our swimwear at the beach, and then started the climb in our newly-purchased water shoes.

About halfway up, I began to lose stamina. My breathing became labored and I could go no further. Ursula was already a ways ahead of me, so I sat down beside the falls to catch my breath.

When my breathing became normal again, I slowly finished the climb to the top.

Ursula made me promise to see my cardiologist as soon as we were back in Detroit; which I did.

He diagnosed me with congestive heart failure and in short order performed an angioplasty at the Saint Joseph hospital on 19 Mile Road to open up some of the arteries surrounding my heart. Afterwards, on doctors' orders, I recuperated with a few weeks at home.

As I wind down the story of how plastics became the automotive material of choice used on American cars during my 30 years with the industry, I have one more interesting little story to tell.

When I returned to the office I received a call from my good friend Guenther Troester in Germany. He confided that Fiat in Brescia, Italy intended to sell their plastic parts molding plant for their IVECO trucks. I talked to Richard and we agreed it was worth investigating.

I called Fiat and found someone with knowledge of this development. He told me it was still a big secret, "you know," and not to discuss it with anyone! He asked if I could come to Brescia to talk with someone who would be authorized to talk about it.

I agreed, flew to Frankfurt and then on to Turin, rented a car and made the first of many drives to the Brescia plant. We arranged a meeting for the following morning at 10:00 am.

I met with Mario, an engineer, who took me to the molding area located at the rear of the truck plant. It was perfectly located, right at the site, adjacent to where the plastic parts were assembled right to the chassis.

The molding plant was in immaculate condition, full of the most modern equipment and very clean. Everything was laid out precisely, with raw materials, then the molding, decorating and finishing processes – all with efficient material-flow in mind.

I watched all the processes, from the mat, molding and processing, and checking product for most of the day and could find no fault. This plant was the most modern thermoset processing plant that money could buy!

I conveyed to Mario my impression of how great everything looked, how functional it was, and how good the quality of the finished parts were.

And I could tell how proud he was. I found out later that he had been the one in charge of redesigning and rebuilding the plant from a previous, less efficient molding plant.

A meeting was arranged for the following morning, again at 10:00 a.m. (I think Italians don't like early morning meetings, and that was OK with me because I was then able to spend the early part of the day seeing the city and the surrounding area in daylight.)

Next morning I was met by two executives in a big, beautifully well lit conference room, with a huge mahogany table set up with coffee, cold sparkling water, and cookies. Through the huge windows I could see the Alps in the background.

What a setting for a conference room! It was more like being in one of the most expensive wellness hotels. I could tell that old Italian (Agnelli) money had been spent lavishly there.

After the greetings were done Guido, the senior negotiator, asked for my thoughts about the molding plant.

I told him that I thought it was an absolutely beautiful plant, but that it was, quite obviously, losing a lot of money every day because it was underutilized producing parts for their trucks alone, and on a just-in-time basis. It also was staffed with too many highly-paid people for what was being required of it.

He did not like my comments, but he also did not say I was wrong.

I told him what the plant desperately needed was additional work, and that the plastics plant needed to be separated from the truck plant so it could utilize lower paid staff, in line with the wage scale at similar plastic-processing plants.

There was no argument from their side. I could tell they were not hearing anything they had not thought about themselves. But I could also tell that they did not like to hear it from an American stranger!

I told them that, under the right circumstances, Cambridge could help with this problem. We talked a little bit more about it without going into details. After lunch, I called Diane to get me back to Detroit.

Back home, Richard and I considered how we could proceed, knowing that Kevin and his operations crew would not want to participate in a European venture. But we also knew that this was another golden opportunity to be a force in Europe.

I was sure that if we approached this the right way, we could get the Brescia molding plant with little or no monetary investment.

The biggest problem we would encounter would be separating the molding plant from the rest of the truck facility.

We decided to string them along to see how things would turn out, both here in the U.S. with Cambridge and with the development of the plastics industry in Europe.

I called the executive in charge at Fiat a few days later to show mild interest and we agreed to a follow up meeting. I could tell that they were eager to continue talking.

At the second meeting I assured them we could come to terms, but warned that separating the molding plant from the truck plant was entirely in their hands and needed to be done in order to seal the deal.

They assured me that they were working with their labor unions and wanted to pursue the sale. I flew back and forth at least 6 more times, during which period most of the year went by.

I used the time in Europe to visit the car and truck producers, as well as our joint-venture partners, to get work into the plant. (I also stocked up on real Italian silk ties, which I purchased at a specialty shop at the Turin Airport.)

By years end, I had received promises from three companies to put work into the Brescia molding plant and received an agreement-in-principle that Cambridge could have the molding plant for the proverbial "one-dollar" sum.

That was the good part.

Separating the molding plant from the truck plant continued to be the problem. The union adamantly refused to give up its members. They wanted things to remain as they were, with all the current members in the "new Cambridge plant" and with the current wage structure. I was not privy to the meetings with the unions, but I flew home and back to Italy quite a few times.

In the end, the union won. They would not allow the separation under the terms that we specified and needed in order to run the plant successfully and profitably.

This was a definite deal breaker.

To this day the plastic plant continues to produce all the plastic parts for Fiat IVECO trucks only, at the higher cost.

But consider also that all manufacturing costs associated with building the truck are buried in the final selling price of the completed vehicle. And, for what it's worth, the new trucks look better with molded-plastic parts and are still being produced cheaper than they were 10, 20 or 30 years ago when steel was the only material available for the outer skin!

CHAPTER 18: Almost All Plastic

And that holds true for every car, SUV, and truck manufactured anywhere in the world today.

Without the technical contributions of plastics, today's vehicles would just lumber along, too heavy to be fuel-efficient; and they would be far more expensive than they are today!

Let's take a look at the only non-plastic parts left on a vehicle today – bearing in mind that the first two of these big systems have many moving plastic parts inside and around them – the:

1. Engine block
2. Transmission housing
3. Drive shaft and differential with axle
4. Radiator
5. Muffler and exhaust pipes
6. Some metal body panels still used on some cars, (to keep the steel industry happy)
7. Torsion bars or shocks
8. Wheels

9. Glass (except for the layer of plastic inside the safety glass of the windshield and on the windows
10. All those little electric motors with the copper wires that are all over today's cars, and
11. Chassis

All other parts, in one way or another, can and/or are now being made and used on models somewhere in the world with some type of plastic. Not on every model yet, but time is on plastic's side.

I know for a fact that tests are ongoing to replace the driveshaft, the torsion bars, and the wheels and it is only a matter of time before the change to plastics can be safely made. Wheels, drive shafts and torsion bars – and let's not forget tubing – are being tested for their potential as plastic parts as I write this.

Cheaper oil and natural gas prices keep plastic costs down and drive the development of stronger, more versatile, and more heat-resistant plastic materials.

Most exterior parts used on vehicles produced all over the world today, including bumper systems, are made with plastic.

Just think – there is no longer a steel bumper factory-installed on any car model made!

The entire interior of vehicles produced today is made with some type of plastic material.

There are very few parts that the plastics industry cannot duplicate, and very important, make lighter and make cheaper.

3D printing has now eliminated the time-consuming process of model building and try-outs with prototype parts. Small production runs are now made utilizing only 3D printing!

CHAPTER 19: Glastic, the Last Hurrah

My being away most of the year had given Kevin Alder many opportunities to talk to Richard and convince him to stop trying to expand Cambridge in Europe and, for that matter, anywhere else in the world.

Due to the constant pricing pressures from our customers and a variety of internal reasons, Cambridge was starting to lose money, and Kevin warned that the company was struggling with the workload we had, to the point where he was forced to refuse work from some of our customers.

At the same time, our Centralia Plant had problems producing a spoiler to BMW's quality standards. Our Centralia people simply would not buy into BMW's higher standards. 'If it is good enough for the U.S. it has to be good enough for BMW,' was the official response!

To settle the matter, and assure a problem-free start-up at BMW's Spartanburg plant, we decided to fly the spoiler tools to our joint-venture partner in Germany, Menzolit, and produce the parts there.

This increased the cost considerably due to the parts now being produced in Bretten and then having to be shipped from Germany to Spartanburg.

That was not the development I wanted.

BMW was unhappy with Cambridge and Menzolit was unhappy because they had to make room for the spoiler production. Centralia blamed me, and BMW's unreasonable quality demands! Everybody was unhappy!

In March 1999, Kevin told Richard that he had to reduce Cambridge's overhead in order to contain losses. He prepared a list of non-essential employees to be eliminated.

Terry and I were on that list!

Terry and I met with Richard the next day, at which time he told us not to worry, that he had been thinking of selling Cambridge for awhile, and that he'd had a number of secret talks with another company.

In the meantime, he suggested that we should look for a company in our area that was for sale, and that the three of us could acquire it if it proved suitable.

In order for me to accept the departure from Cambridge, Kevin had prepared a decent severance package, which I did accept.

But again, for the third time now, I was looking for new employment.

The difference was that I was now 63 years old.

The following week, Terry and I were set up at our corporate attorney's office, where we started to hunt for a suitable acquisition. I have to say that there were quite a number available.

One of our requirements was that it must be within a mile of the automotive suppliers. We'd all had our fill with long distances to transport parts!!!

About a month later, Richard called and told me that he had come to terms with the other company and was in the process of selling Cambridge.

It was yet another company I had seen from its infancy to an undeserved end.

By July we had narrowed our search and focused on the Glastic Corporation, a plastic thermo set molder producing parts for the electrical business community.

Some of the products were high-voltage overland insulators, old-fashioned fuses (they produced over 2 million every year), insulation sheets for the electrical motor industry, and miles and miles of optical fibers.

The company had been established in 1942 in Cleveland, Ohio, and had been privately held until 1990 when it was sold to the Kobe Steel Corporation of Japan. Kobe had purchased it with the hope of establishing a beachhead in the U.S.

Unfortunately, the management they brought to the U.S. knew nothing about plastics and its related businesses, and they lost money from the start. Nine years later, although then under a different management, Kobe decided to cut their losses and offered Glastic for sale.

We negotiated and came to an agreement with them in November, and signed the sales documents on the 5th of December 1999.

Terry became vice president of manufacturing, I was vice president of sales, and Richard was the silent partner. Terry and I agreed to alternate the president and vice president positions on a yearly basis.

I was still in the plastics business, but for the first time – and thankfully – I was no longer associated with the automotive industry.

The plant was in need of a big cleanup and the people needed to be reeducated in our ways of doing business. We interviewed the staff and weeded out the nonperformers. The plant had been seriously overstaffed and we took care of that.

Terry was up for the task of turning the plant around to be an efficient, smooth-running factory and I used my considerable sales experience. I visited all Glastic's customers during the first two months, promising them both better quality and better service.

Working together, we managed to keep these promises and, as a result, our sales quickly increased and we were in the black by the end of May of that year (less than 6 months!)

Terry and I rented separate apartments in a very nice Cleveland suburb.

My apartment was a beautiful place on a little lake on the outskirts of Cleveland. I stayed there during the week and drove back to Detroit every Friday afternoon to spend the weekends with Ursula.

This arrangement was fine until September 20, 2001 right on my 65th birthday, when I had a heart attack during the night. I drove myself to the Cleveland Hospital at 4:00 in the morning.

Thank God, I recovered nicely in the hospital after a stent was placed into one of my heart arteries.

But, having time to lie around in my hospital bed and think, I decided that the time had come to work on my retirement plans. I talked to Richard about hiring a sales manager who, with my help, would take over my sales responsibilities. He agreed and I hired Mark. I had run into Mark a number of times and liked how he handled himself.

For myself, I set up an office at my home in Detroit. We had a pretty good IT guy, and he set me up, assuring me that I would be connected to the Cleveland office 24 hours a day.

I still had control of the sales strategy, but I left the travelling and customer visits, and the daily stress, to Mark and others.

So during the course of the next year or two I passed on more and more of the sales and marketing responsibility to Mark, as it became apparent that I had made a good hire.

Remembering how I hated Mike Ladney's interference from afar back in 1984, I promised myself not to do that. Ever!

Some six years later, on January 15, 2007, an opportunity arose and Richard, Terry, and I sold Glastic to the Roechling Corporation of Germany.

I had known Roechling, met its president years earlier through Otto, and had had a few meetings at their headquarters in Manheim. Afterwards, we continued a friendly relationship through phone calls while I was at Cambridge and Glastic.

Not a month later I started to have chest pains again and my cardiologist suggested – this time – a triple bypass operation.

It was performed successfully at the Henry Ford Hospital in Detroit and, again, I recovered very nicely. I have not had any heart problems since then.

I watch what I eat now, but I still carry a bit more weight with me than I should.

Every once in awhile I miss the thrill that I felt being part of the plastics revolution - introducing a new application for a plastic part or product to the automotive community.

And, as silly as it sounds, I still miss the smell associated with plastic pellets being melted and formed into an automotive part!

Epilogue

In December of 2015 we celebrated the college graduation of Rebecca Amatangelo, my second oldest granddaughter, at Piccerilis, one of our favorite Italian restaurants. Two of our grandchildren have now successfully finished college; there are three more to go.

I am enjoying my retirement now and Ursula and I continue to travel a lot. We have begun to spend the winters in Fort Myer, Florida. As I have gotten older I increasingly dislike the frigid Michigan winters and look for a warmer climate during January and February.

Richard moved his office to Naples, Florida and lives and still works there. He looked good as always, still working at 69. We talked for about an hour and promised each other to stay in touch.

I had planned to visit Terry in Venice. He retired and built a house on a golf course there. Unfortunately the visits did not materialize, as timing (his golf matches) and distance made it impossible to connect our schedules.

Mike Ladney died in April 2016 in Port Huron, Michigan, a town about 50 miles north of Detroit.

Just south of Port Huron in Marysville was where he'd built the polypropylene plant with the Chinese and Canadian partners back in 1987, bringing feedstock via a pipeline from Sarnia and across the Saint Clair River to make polypropylene. Nobody knows how or why he ended up back there! He was 96 years old when he died.

Rumor has it that Mike had married his housekeeper, a woman from Guatemala, and that he lost his memory to dementia – also, that the new wife took all his money and went back to her homeland. But that is just a rumor!

Marguerite Ladney is still alive at 100. She is living at an assisted living home in Birmington, Michigan, and has plans to become at least 107 years old to beat the record of an aunt who died at 106.

She continues to be a classy lady and talks with great accuracy about the good times we had at DPM. She also remembers how hard we all worked to achieve the company's successes.

Ursula bakes sugar cookies for her and I take them over and talk with her every week or so. Once a month I drive her to the stylist in Grosse Point to have her hair done. We discuss politics; she has been a lifelong member and financial supporter of the Republican Party, and she follows the political developments on Fox News on most days.

I also stay in touch with her daughter, Carol Ann, who has taken charge of her well being and now takes care of her and her two cats.

And I still miss the smell of plastic being heated and processed into beautiful automotive parts!